W9-BZB-679

EX-Libris: Friends of
Lake County Public Library

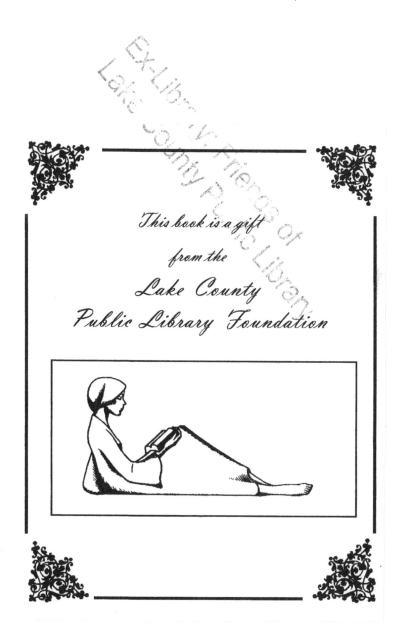

This book is a gift

from the

Lake County
Public Library Foundation

JUNIOR DRUG AWARENESS

Diet Pills

JUNIOR DRUG AWARENESS

JUNIOR DRUG AWARENESS

Diet Pills

Amy E. Breguet

LAKE COUNTY PUBLIC LIBRARY

CHELSEA HOUSE
PUBLISHERS
An imprint of Infobase Publishing

Junior Drug Awareness: Diet Pills
Copyright © 2009 by Infobase Publishing

All rights reserved. No part of this book may be reproduced or utilized in
any form or by any means, electronic or mechanical, including photocopying,
recording, or by any information storage or retrieval systems, without permission
in writing from the publisher. For information contact:

Chelsea House
An imprint of Infobase Publishing
132 West 31st Street
New York NY 10001

3 3113 02763 1557

Library of Congress Cataloging-in-Publication Data

Breguet, Amy.
  Diet pills / by Amy E. Breguet.
      p. cm. — (Junior drug awarenes)
  Includes bibliographical references and index.
  ISBN 978-0-7910-9750-2 (hardcover)
  1. Appetite depressants—Juvenile literature. I. Title. II. Series.

  RM332.3.B74 2009
  615'.78—dc22   2008014068

Chelsea House books are available at special discounts when purchased in
bulk quantities for businesses, associations, institutions, or sales promotions.
Please call our Special Sales Department in New York at (212) 967-8800 or
(800) 322-8755.

You can find Chelsea House on the World Wide Web
at http://www.chelseahouse.com

Text design by Erik Lindstrom
Cover design by Jooyoung An

Printed in the United States

Bang NMSG 10 9 8 7 6 5 4 3 2 1

This book is printed on acid-free paper.

All links and web addresses were checked and verified to be correct at the time of
publication. Because of the dynamic nature of the web, some addresses and links
may have changed since publication and may no longer be valid.

CONTENTS

Battling a Pandemic: A History of Drugs in the United States

When Johnny came marching home again after the Civil War, he probably wasn't marching in a very straight line. This is because Johnny, like 400,000 of his fellow drug-addled soldiers, was addicted to morphine. With the advent of morphine and the invention of the hypodermic needle, drug addiction became a prominent problem during the nineteenth century. It was the first time such widespread drug dependence was documented in history.

Things didn't get much better in the later decades of the nineteenth century. Cocaine and opiates were used as over-the-counter "medicines." Of course, the most famous was Coca-Cola, which actually did contain cocaine in its early days.

After the turn of the twentieth century, drug abuse was spiraling out of control, and the United States government stepped in with the first regulatory controls. In 1906, the Pure Food and Drug Act became a law. It required the labeling of product ingredients. Next came the Harrison Narcotics Tax Act of 1914, which outlawed illegal importation or distribution of cocaine and opiates. During this time, neither the medical community nor the general population was aware of the principles of addiction.

After the passage of the Harrison Act, drug addiction was not a major issue in the United States until the 1960s, when drug abuse became a much bigger social problem. During this time, the federal government's drug enforcement agencies were found to be ineffective. Organizations often worked against one another, causing counterproductive effects. By 1973, things had gotten so bad that President Richard Nixon, by executive order, created the Drug Enforcement Administration (DEA), which became the lead agency in all federal narcotics investigations. It continues in that role to this day. The effectiveness of enforcement and the so-called "Drug War" are open to debate. Cocaine use has been reduced by 75% since its peak in 1985. However, its replacement might be methamphetamine (speed, crank, crystal), which is arguably more dangerous and is now plaguing the country. Also, illicit drugs tend to be cyclical, with various drugs, such as LSD, appearing, disappearing, and then reappearing again. It is probably closest to the truth to say that a war on drugs can never be won, just managed.

Fighting drugs involves a three-pronged battle. Enforcement is one prong. Education and prevention is the second. Treatment is the third.

Although pandemics of drug abuse have been with us for more than 150 years, education and prevention were not seriously considered until the 1970s. In 1982, former First Lady Betty Ford made drug treatment socially acceptable with the opening of the Betty Ford Center. This followed her own battle with addiction. Other treatment centers—including Hazelden, Fair Oaks, and Smithers (now called the Addiction Institute of New York)—added to the growing number of clinics, and soon detox facilities were in almost every city. The cost of a single day in one of these facilities is often more than $1,000, and the effectiveness of treatment centers is often debated. To this day, there is little regulation over who can practice counseling.

It soon became apparent that the most effective way to deal with the drug problem was prevention by education. By some estimates, the overall cost of drug abuse to society exceeds $250 billion per year; preventive education is certainly the most cost-effective way to deal with the problem. Drug education can save people from misery, pain, and ultimately even jail time or death. In the early 1980s, First Lady Nancy Reagan started the "Just Say No" program. Although many scoffed at the program, its promotion of total abstinence from drugs has been effective with many adolescents. In the late 1980s, drug education was not science-based, and people essentially were throwing mud at the wall to see what would stick. Motivations of all types spawned hundreds, if not thousands, of drug-education programs. Promoters of some programs used whatever political clout they could muster to get on various government agencies' lists of most effective programs. The bottom line, however, is that prevention is very difficult to quantify. It's nearly impossible to prove that drug use would have occurred if it were not prevented from happening.

In 1983, the Los Angeles Unified School District, in conjunction with the Los Angeles Police Department, started what was considered at that time to be the gold standard of school-based drug education programs. The program was called Drug Abuse Resistance Education, otherwise known as D.A.R.E. The program called for specially trained police officers to deliver drug-education programs in schools. This was an era in which community-oriented policing was all the rage. The logic was that kids would give street credibility to a police officer who spoke to them about drugs. The popularity of the program was unprecedented. It spread all across the country and around the world. Ultimately, 80% of American school districts would utilize the program. Parents, police officers, and kids all loved it. Unexpectedly, a special bond was formed between the kids who took the program and the police officers who ran it. Even in adulthood, many kids remember the name of their D.A.R.E. officer.

By 1991, national drug use had been halved. In any other medical-oriented field, this figure would be astonishing. The number of people in the United States using drugs went from about 25 million in the early 1980s to 11 million in 1991. All three prongs of the battle against drugs vied for government dollars, with each prong claiming credit for the reduction in drug use. There is no doubt that each contributed to the decline in drug use, but most people agreed that preventing drug abuse before it started had proved to be the most effective strategy. The National Institute on Drug Abuse (NIDA), which was established in 1974, defines its mandate in this way: "NIDA's mission is to lead the Nation in bringing the power of science to bear on drug abuse and addiction." NIDA leaders were the experts in prevention and treatment, and they had enormous resources. In

1986, the nonprofit Partnership for a Drug-Free America was founded. The organization defined its mission as, "Putting to use all major media outlets, including TV, radio, print advertisements and the Internet, along with the pro bono work of the country's best advertising agencies." The Partnership for a Drug-Free America is responsible for the popular campaign that compared "your brain on drugs" to fried eggs.

The American drug problem was front-page news for years up until 1990–1991. Then the Gulf War took over the news, and drugs never again regained the headlines. Most likely, this lack of media coverage has led to some peaks and valleys in the number of people using drugs, but there has not been a return to anything near the high percentage of use recorded in 1985. According to the University of Michigan's 2006 Monitoring the Future study, which measured adolescent drug use, there were 840,000 fewer American kids using drugs in 2006 than in 2001. This represents a 23% reduction in drug use. With the exception of prescription drugs, drug use continues to decline.

In 2000, the Robert Wood Johnson Foundation recognized that the D.A.R.E. Program, with its tens of thousands of trained police officers, had the top state-of-the-art delivery system of drug education in the world. The foundation dedicated $15 million to develop a cutting-edge prevention curriculum to be delivered by D.A.R.E. The new D.A.R.E. program incorporates the latest in prevention and education, including high-tech, interactive, and decision-model-based approaches. D.A.R.E. officers are trained as "coaches" who support kids as they practice research-based refusal strategies in high-stakes peer-pressure environments. Through stunning magnetic resonance imaging (MRI) images, students get to see tangible proof of how various substances diminish brain activity.

Will this program be the solution to the drug problem in the United States? By itself, probably not. It is simply an integral part of a larger equation that everyone involved hopes will prevent kids from ever starting to use drugs. The equation also requires guidance in the home, without which no program can be effective.

Ronald J. Brogan
Regional Director
D.A.R.E. America

Weight-Obsessed Culture

The issue of weight—too much, too little, needing to lose it, or needlessly trying to lose it—is a constant concern in American culture. The primary message is that, to be beautiful, happy, and loved, a person needs to lose weight. Many people place the blame for this message on advertising images and other media, such as television shows and movies. It is clearly a false and destructive idea. The fact is, about two-thirds of Americans *would* benefit from being fitter and healthier, but for reasons that have nothing to do with beauty or love. According to medical guidelines, many people who are considered overweight can reduce certain health risks and feel better all around by getting in shape and improving their diets.

According to several studies and surveys, most Americans, for one reason or another, have weight loss on the brain. And that has meant billions of dollars in business for the weight loss industry.

OBESITY ON THE RISE

Generally speaking, Americans weigh more than ever before. According to the Weight-control Information Network of the National Institutes of Health, the number of people who are overweight has increased more than 20% since 1960. The number of people who are obese (extremely overweight) has skyrocketed more than 50%. Why the increase? Researchers point to growing portion sizes in restaurants, as well as people eating more fast food and having less active lifestyles.

This trend hasn't only affected adults. A record number of children and teens are struggling with weight problems as well. About 17% of children and teens (ages 6 to 19) are currently overweight. Genetics, family environment, and eating habits have likely played a role in these numbers. Lack of physical activity, however, is something of special concern among experts. "I often think about how different things were 20 years ago when kids were outside playing sports and burning **calories** instead of sitting inside playing video games on the computer," said nutritionist Dr. Bob Keith of the Alabama Cooperative Extension System (ACES) at the University of Alabama. He discussed his thoughts on physical activity among teens in an interview for the ACES Web site. "What you have is a generation that has to make an effort to be physically active."

Above average weight or obesity can be the cause of multiple health problems, including diabetes, heart

McDonald's introduced a fruit and walnut salad in 2005 in an effort to offer healthier items on their menu. Researchers believe that fast food restaurants, such as McDonald's and Burger King, play a major role in Americans' weight gain.

disease, stroke, some cancers, liver problems, osteoar-thritis (pain in the joints), and sleep apnea (periods of stopped breathing during sleep). For these reasons, it is important to stay active and eat right to protect overall health. If a person thinks he or she may need to lose weight for health reasons, a doctor will help that person safely start and maintain a healthy lifestyle. Read on to learn why a diet pill or other weight loss product will likely *not* be part of the plan.

BMI: BEYOND THE SCALE

Overweight and *obese* are medical terms. The body mass index, or BMI, is a tool that health-care professionals use to determine if a person's weight could lead to health risks. A person's BMI is calculated using his or her height and weight. The result suggests whether the person is under-weight, overweight, obese, or at a healthy weight. The way BMI is calculated for children and teens differs slightly from the adult BMI in that it takes age and gender into consideration.

Keep in mind that BMI has its limitations. For exam-ple, since muscle weighs more than fat, an athlete may have a higher BMI than a sedentary (inactive) person, even though the athlete is in better shape. Talk to your doctor about *any* questions or concerns you have about your health, especially if you are considering trying to lose weight.

To learn more about BMI and to calculate your own, go to www.kidshealth.org/parent/nutrition_fit/nutrition/ bmi_charts.html or http://www.cdc.gov/nccdphp/ dnpa/bmi.

"YOU NEVER FEEL LIKE YOU'RE THIN ENOUGH"

In addition to increasing numbers of overweight people, there is a surprisingly large number of people who are at a healthy weight but don't believe it. Many of these people are female. According to survey results reported on HealthyPlace.com Mental Health Communities, 75% of women who are at a healthy weight think they are overweight. A 2001 survey of college sorority members found that 86% of them wanted to lose at least a few pounds. These beliefs are not just limited to adult women. In one study published in the 1990s in the *Journal of the American Dietetic Association*, more than half of fourth-grade girls expressed a desire to be thinner.

WHAT'S GOING ON?

For starters, it doesn't help that many stars in movies and television, singers, and other people popularized by the media are thinner than the average American. And these celebrities are often described as having "perfect" bodies. Images of extremely skinny people fill magazine ads, music videos, and popular TV shows. Seeing these images repeated over and over makes them seem normal. The National Institute on Media and the Family reports several studies that say young people feel bad about themselves and angry about the pressure to have a "perfect" body. After seeing images of thin celebrities so often in their daily lives, they begin to believe that this type of body is what is normal. They believe it is realistic and possible to have—and if they don't have it themselves, they think there's something wrong with them.

The way you feel about your body—called your *body image*—is often a big part of how you feel about yourself. Many things affect body image, including media images. It is also affected by an idea that many of today's teens,

(continues on page 20)

Actress Keira Knightley, seen here at award show in 2008, has often come under fire from the media for looking too thin. The actress has consistently denied having an eating disorder and successfully sued the UK tabloid the *Daily Mail* in 2007 over an article that suggested her physique and her refusal to admit to an eating disorder were to blame for the anorexia-related death of a 19-year-old girl.

WEIGHT-OBSESSED MALES: A GROWING POPULATION

Many people think that body image, weight obsession, and eating disorders are "girl things." Think again. It's true that these issues are more common among females. But a growing number of boys and men are buying into media and cultural messages that may lead them to unhealthy attempts to control weight, shape, and size.

Most males who are worried about their appearance don't want to look stick-thin. They aspire to have a lot of muscle and little fat. "It's just that when you look at TV shows, everyone that's successful has a six-pack [muscular stomach]," said Charlie Mileski, a 19-year-old who spoke to ABC News. The station interviewed him for a 2006 feature on the rising number of males suffering from anorexia nervosa, an eating disorder that involves strict control of eating.

Whether skinny or extremely muscular, the physical appearance that so many females and males seek is a dangerous and nearly impossible goal. Charlie Mileski was diagnosed with anorexia at age 14. He would run seven miles a day and count calories obsessively in order to control his weight. Said his father, Joe Mileski: "He told me there are 24 calories in licking a postage stamp." Within three months, Charlie Mileski had plummeted from 150 pounds to 104. He was 5 foot 10 inches at the time. He entered a treatment program and has learned to be more comfortable with his body, but he still struggles to stay healthy. "Half the time I'm satisfied with my body," he said. "And half the time I can just throw up at the sight of it."

The desire among boys to be buff is so common and dangerous that experts have given it a name: muscle

Though commonly associated with females, pressure about weight and body image is affecting a growing number of males. A strong desire to be bigger and stronger causes many young males to go to unhealthy extremes to attain what they believe is the perfect look.

dysmorphia. Sometimes it might also be called "bigorexia," a play on the word *anorexia*. Just as some people may look in the mirror and see their underweight bodies as fat, boys may see a body that completely lacks muscle tone. Psychiatry professor Harrison G. Pope and his co-authors describe this disorder in the 2002 book *The Adonis Complex: How to Identify, Treat and Prevent Body Obsession in Men and Boys*. Some experts warn that this warped view of one's own body leads many teenage boys to

(continues on page 20)

(continued from page 19)

engage in daily, obsessive weight-training sessions, strict rules about eating, or worse.

It is clear that boys are not safe from the pressures to look a certain way. "We have done a scam job on boys," William Pollack, author of *Real Boys: Rescuing Our Sons From the Myth of Boyhood* and *Real Boys' Voices,* told the *Oakland Tribune.* "We have told them, in essence, that they are not truly masculine unless they look a certain way."

(continued from page 16)

especially girls, seem to have: that they need to be "perfect" all around. "There are so many pressures of being a teenage girl," wrote a ninth-grader who participated in The Supergirl Dilemma: Girls Grapple with the Mounting Pressure of Expectations, a 2006 study by Girls, Inc. "You never feel like you're thin enough, pretty enough, or just good enough." This type of thinking can lead a person to be extremely strict with himself or herself, especially in the area of weight control. Some girls (and boys) may believe that if they could just look like a celebrity, model, or sports star, everything else would fall into place. They may develop eating disorders or abuse products they think will help them lose weight. And that's where serious physical and emotional danger begins.

PROGRAMS, PILLS, AND PROMISES

Millions of Americans want to slim down, whether they are actually overweight or just somehow feel that they are. There is no shortage of weight loss products and programs that claim to help. There are special diets, weight loss centers, private diet counselors, even surgeries—and, of course, pills. All weight loss products and programs cost something, whether it's the price of a book that outlines what to eat, or a membership that provides guidance and meals. In some cases, all people end up losing is money and optimism.

If a person crosses the line from improving nutrition and fitness to using drugs or supplements, many advertisements claim he or she can lose even more. At that point, dieting becomes a health hazard. The U.S. Food and Drug Administration (FDA) is the government agency that watches and controls food and medical products that are sold to consumers. Before medical products can be sold, the FDA must approve them. The FDA has not approved any diet pills claiming to be weight loss miracles. In order to be approved, a product must be proven safe and effective. No company has yet proven that its diet pills are either of these things. Unfortunately, many consumers put their faith in diet pills anyway. The weight loss product business is expected to make $61 billion per year by 2008. Of that amount, more than $700 million is expected to come from sales of **over-the-counter (OTC)** diet pills.

The term *diet pill* can be used today to describe several products. It might be a prescription medicine (a medicine that is only available through a doctor, and there are a few), a "formula," or one of countless herbal supplements. The selection of diet pills wasn't always as wide as it is today. The first real weight loss drug, containing a chemical called dinitrophenol (DNP), was developed in the 1930s. It caused a person's body to sweat out extra calories rather than storing them as fat. The drug was originally developed to help people who were very overweight. But it soon became available to

Weight loss programs and products have flooded the market in the last few decades. Most are not tested or approved by the FDA.

everyone. DNP was quickly pulled from the market, after it was shown to cause blindness and even death among people who became overheated.

In the 1950s another type of diet pill was introduced, called amphetamines. These act as stimulants, which means they speed up the processes that go on in the body. They work by decreasing a person's appetite, which reduces the urge to eat. They also raise **metabolism**. Amphetamines often result in weight loss, but at a price: Long-term use sometimes causes paranoia, mood swings, and high blood pressure, among other problems. People found that when they stopped taking the drugs, they rapidly gained weight and became depressed.

Amphetamines became increasingly less popular as diet supplements, and eventually the FDA reversed its approval of them as weight loss drugs.

Other drugs were developed. Some—including "fen-phen" (fenfluramine and phentermine) and drugs containing the stimulant **ephedra**—initially enjoyed raging popularity. Yet, they too were later banned due to serious health risks.

By the late 1990s, herbal **supplements** became more popular and were promoted for the prevention and treatment of nearly any physical problem or concern. Weight loss was no exception. In fact, most OTC diet pills now contain an herb or combination of an herb and another substance.

Of all the weight loss options available, pills are the one that seem the simplest. They are also one of the riskiest.

Appetite Suppressants

Americans have been using manufactured drugs to reduce or eliminate hunger in order to lose weight for more than 50 years. The first of these kinds of drugs, amphetamines, was actually first marketed for nasal congestion. However, it wasn't long before companies began making and advertising drugs just for this purpose.

THE DAYS OF DEXATRIM

Call it the original diet pill. The introduction of the OTC appetite suppressant Dexatrim in 1976 marked the beginning of an era in the history of dieting trends. The pill's main ingredient was phenylpropanolamine (PPA). This substance works by affecting the hypothalamus—the part

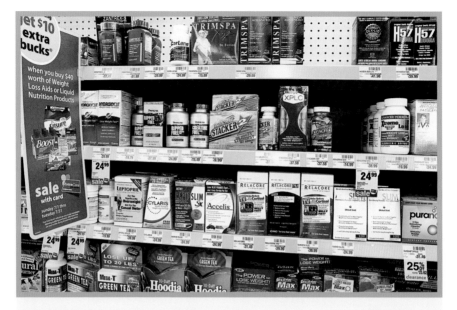

A CVS Pharmacy in Los Angeles displays various brands of diet pills.

of the brain that controls hunger, among other functions. PPA seemed to work for many people. The popularity of Dexatrim and similar drugs, especially Acutrim, skyrocketed and remained steady into the early 1990s.

As happens with so many "miracle" ingredients, experts eventually discovered that PPA had a possible dark side. A 2000 study by the Yale University School of Medicine found that PPA increases the risk of hemorrhagic stroke, which is a kind of stroke caused when blood vessels in the brain start to bleed. In response to this finding, the U.S. Food and Drug Administration (FDA) immediately warned consumers not to use any drugs containing PPA. This included some cough and cold medicines. The FDA also asked companies to remove the ingredient from their products. Many manufacturers, including the company that made Dexatrim, agreed to the request. However, the steps necessary to legally ban a drug take years to complete.

As a result, Dexatrim is still available today, although it is not as popular as it used to be. The company that makes Dexatrim has changed its recipe several times. The Web site called the Diet Channel compared Dexatrim to a chameleon, a kind of lizard that changes the color of its skin to blend into its surroundings. The pills now mainly contain herbal ingredients, which are growing more and

CIGARETTES AND WEIGHT LOSS

Despite the well-known, fatal dangers of smoking, teens nationwide continue to try it every day. Unfortunately, many of them will become addicted and lead unhealthy lives because of it.

Surveys show many reasons why people claim to first try smoking, including peer pressure, wanting to look older, and trying to be like a celebrity who smokes. Many teen magazines and Web sites, however, note that the number one reason teenage girls start smoking is to lose weight.

While it's true that the nicotine (the addictive drug in cigarettes) may **suppress** a person's appetite, that fact doesn't mean it will lead to weight loss. Smoking has never been proven as a successful weight loss strategy. For one thing, people who smoke often do little or nothing to stay fit. A study published by the American College of Nutrition found that college students who smoked in an effort to lose weight also tended to eat high-calorie foods and eat more popular these days. This makes Dexatrim similar to most other OTC diet pills marketed in stores today.

DIET PILLS GO HERBAL

It may seem like there is an herb available to cure anything that ails you. Herbal pills and other dietary supplements claim to provide a solution for everything from memory problems to frequent colds. Supplement companies have a pill for weight loss, too.

in front of the TV. In addition, regular exercise is likely to be a problem. This is because smoking makes it difficult to breathe deeply. It's hard for a person to be active when he or she is gasping for breath after only a few minutes of jogging or playing a sport.

A 2007 Australian study on animals came up with this further breaking news: Smoking may actually cause the body to store extra fat. In the study, mice that were exposed to nicotine ate less but did not lose weight. The study's findings suggested that when humans lose any weight from smoking, they are probably losing the weight of muscle and organ tissue, not fat. "I think the message from this study is that using smoking to suppress body weight gain, if you're overweight, is not going to be helpful," said researcher Margaret Morris, a pharmacology professor at the University of New South Wales. The broader message is that cigarettes are good for nothing.

The FDA does not approve dietary supplements. This means that, regardless of what supplement labels or advertisements may say, the safety and effectiveness of supplements has not been proven. "You really don't know what you're getting when you buy some of these products," said Cynthia Sass, of the American Dietetic Association, to ABC News for a 2006 story on weight loss supplements. "You don't know if what's in there is what it says. You don't know if it's going to be safe, you don't know if it's going to work. You don't know what kind of side effects it's going to have." For these reasons, people should talk to their doctors before taking any kind of dietary supplement—for weight loss or anything else.

As with medicines, different supplements may aim to address the same problem from various angles. For example, acetaminophen and ibuprofen both work on pain, but they target different brain and body functions to do so. In the same way, not all supplements claim to lead to weight loss in the same way. Supplements designed mainly to lessen appetite usually contain an herbal ingredient called hoodia.

Hoodia (full name: *hoodia gordonii*) is native to the South African desert. It is a member of the *Asclepiadaceae* plant family and resembles a cactus. Hoodia acts like glucose (blood sugar) in the body. Because of this, it can trick the brain into thinking the body has eaten. When this happens, a person does not feel hungry. This is not natural. The brain gives off hunger signals for a reason: It needs fuel. There's nothing healthy about shutting down hunger pangs.

Hoodia is the active ingredient in most of the popular appetite suppressants available today, including *Hoodia 750, Ethno Africa, Miracle Burn,* and *Hoodia 911.* Many products from TrimSpa also contain hoodia. (TrimSpa once featured Anna Nicole Smith in its ads, boasting that

The FDA does not approve dietary supplements. Many supplements designed to reduce appetite contain hoodia. The hoodia plant has large, fleshy colored flowers that smell like rotten meat. The stinky flowers attract flies to pollinate them. Once the spines have been removed, the stems of the plant are eaten raw or manufactured to be used as appetite suppressants.

she had suddenly lost large amounts of weight after using their products.)

Hoodia is commonly found in pill form, although some brands have also come out with shakes, teas, energy bars, chocolates, and even skin patches. Hoodia only grows naturally in the Kalahari Desert of South Africa. Because of this, finding and processing the plant can be a challenge. That causes the price to go up for products that contain hoodia. Depending on the brand, how many pills the bottle contains, and other factors, an average bottle costs betweem $30 and $60.

Makers and fans of hoodia supplements will often point out that hoodia is not a stimulant. In this way, it is not like many other diet pill ingredients, such as ephe-dra (which is now banned). They argue that this means hoodia is safe. But the truth is that no medicine or sup-plement is safe until scientists prove it is safe. Even then, scientists may later find out that they were wrong.

APPETITE SUPPRESSION BY PRESCRIPTION

These days it is hard to find weight loss drugs that the FDA has approved. But they do exist, mainly behind the pharmacy counter. Scientists are always looking for ways to help people lose weight and avoid certain dis-eases that are linked to poor nutrition and fitness habits. Scientists have found that medicines may be part of the solution.

The two best-known prescription diet pills being sold today are sibutramine (brand name Meridia) and orlistat (Xenical). Sibutramine is an appetite suppres-sant. Orlistat prevents the intestines from absorbing fat. Other medications exist, but they are less common, and people are only supposed to use them for short periods of time.

Some people are looking for a "quick fix" when they go to their doctor for weight loss advice. But no good doctor is going to hand out a diet pill prescription to anyone who wants to lose weight. These drugs are only given to a small number of people. The Mayo Clinic, a world famous medical center located in Minnesota, gives these general rules for deciding who can be given a weight loss drug:

1. The patient has tried other methods of weight loss that haven't worked (and he or she meets one of the following two criteria).
2. The patient's BMI is greater than 27 and he or she has medical problems such as diabetes, high blood pressure, or sleep apnea.

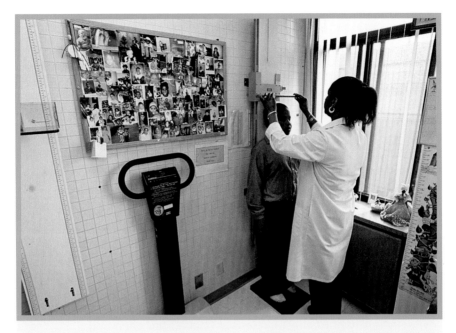

A child is measured and weighed at the Optimal Weight for Life (OWL) Program at the Children's Hospital in Boston in 2000. He lost 5.4 pounds in his first month in the program.

    3.   The patient has a BMI greater than 30.

Even if a doctor decides that weight loss medication may help a patient, it's still no quick fix. Diet and exercise are part of any weight loss program, and the patient is required to follow these measures in addition to taking pills.

It is important to think about the drawbacks of weight loss drugs. For one thing, these drugs are so new that their long-term safety remains largely unknown. Weight loss drugs in the past have been found to cause serious medical problems and, in some cases, death. In general, a patient who is prescribed weight loss drugs needs to take them over a long period of time in order to avoid regaining weight. It often takes a long time to

REMEMBERING FEN-PHEN

In the past, when a promising new weight loss drug was introduced, many Americans rushed to get it. Within a few years, however, new evidence often uncovered serious dangers. One of the most memorable—and disastrous—of these weight loss drugs was a drug known as fen-phen.

Fen-phen was a combination of the drugs fenflura-mine (a mood-changing drug that can help a person feel full) and phentermine (a stimulant diet drug). In 1992, the medical journal *Clinical Pharmacology & Therapeutics* reported the work of Dr. Michael Weintraub of the University of Rochester. He had studied fen-phen and discovered that the combination of the two drugs helped patients lose weight. After Weintraub's discovery, doctors began prescribing the two drugs together even though the combination was not FDA-approved. Once the national media found out about the drug, the demand for fen-phen exploded. It was particularly popular among women. In 1996, fen-phen and a similar, FDA-approved drug called Redux had earned $300 million dollars for the company that made fenfluramine.

Within a year, the craze for fen-phen was more or less over. A study by the Mayo Clinic found that a large percentage of women taking fen-phen were developing serious heart problems. Fen-phen and Redux were quickly taken out of stores. Many people sued the company that made the drugs. The courts agreed to hear only a small number of these cases. The company that made the drugs paid out billions of dollars to the people whom the drugs hurt. Some cases still continue today.

fully understand the effects of taking any weight loss drug for years.

It's not just the long-term effects that cause worry. These drugs have short-term effects, too. For sibutramine, for example, the possible **side effects** include:

- headache
- appetite changes
- runny nose
- nervousness
- chest pain
- vomiting
- mental confusion
- seizures

There is also a long list of drugs that people should not take if they take sibutramine. For example, sibutramine can interact dangerously with blood thinners (such as warfarin), antifungal medications (such as Diflucan), certain antibiotics, certain allergy, cough, and cold medications, HIV drugs, and many drugs for depression or anxiety. And that's just to name a few. In addition, before giving sibutramine to a patient, a doctor needs to know if that person has ever had an eating disorder, a stroke, high blood pressure, a mental disorder, cancer, and many other conditions that possibly can cause problems.

MedlinePlus, an online resource from the National Library of Medicine, states that a person can even become addicted to sibutramine. It's extremely important that patients take this medication exactly as their doctor tells them, and for no longer than a doctor instructs. As with any drug, the risks of sibutramine may outweigh the benefits for many people. It's no simple fix.

3

Fat Burners and Metabolism Boosters

What if you could put the benefits of tough exercise in a pill and sell it? Supplement companies claim to have done just this. Pharmacies, health food stores, and the Internet are flooded with countless products claiming to help the body get rid of fat. So, do they work? As with all supplements, that's an ongoing matter of debate. Fat burners and metabolism boosters are labeled "dietary supplements," since the FDA has yet to approve a medicine for this purpose.

THE THERMOGENIC THEORY

Most of these products supposedly work through **thermogenesis** (or thermogenics). This is the word for the production of heat in the body. This heat process is why lost calories and fat are said to be "burned." The thermogenic weight loss theory has to do with *metabolism,* or the speed at which the body burns fat and calories. The idea is that "turning up the heat" will speed metabolism. Thermogenesis happens naturally through any type of physical activity, including eating. The idea of fat-burning products is to make the process last longer each time the person does physical activity.

Many substances that may have a thermogenic effect are stimulants. The stimulant ephedra, also known as *ma huang,* might be considered the original thermogenic ingredient. Ephedra was widely used in weight loss products and cold medicines before it was banned in 2004 for creating serious health risks. Since then, several other fat-burning supplements have been developed, making new claims to cause weight loss.

BITTER ORANGE: BITTERSWEET AT BEST

An herb called bitter orange has been advertised as the "next best thing" to ephedra. Bitter orange has been used for centuries in traditional Chinese medicine for digestive problems. Today, people looking to lose weight often seek out bitter orange because it includes synephrine. This is a substance similar to ephedra, and it may have thermogenic effects. The problem is that something so closely related to ephedra is bound to have similar dangers. There is already evidence of this being the case.

Like other stimulants, bitter orange can speed up a person's heart and raise his or her blood pressure. According to the National Center for Complimentary and Alternative Medicine (NCCAM), part of the National Institutes of Health, there have been reports of fainting, heart attack, and stroke in people taking either bitter orange alone or in combination with caffeine. People should stay away from this supplement, especially if they have high blood pressure or a heart problem, or if they are taking other supplements (including caffeine) or medicines that may make the heart beat faster.

Beyond these risks, bitter orange also may carry unique dangers because of its effects on metabolism. A 2004 article in *OB/GYN News* warns that taking the herb can interfere with the body's ability to effectively make use of medications. "This introduces a whole new set of problems aside from the stimulant effects," Dr. Sidney Wolfe, director of Public Citizen's Health Research Group, told *OB/GYN News*. "We certainly would not recommend that anyone use this."

The FDA already has felt pressure to take steps toward banning bitter orange, according to the *OB/GYN News* article. U.S. Senator Charles E. Schumer (D-N.Y.) is one person who sent a letter to the agency about it. "It took the FDA more than eight years to go from warning people that ephedra is dangerous to actually banning it," Schumer said in a statement. "In that time, at least 155 people died from it." The National Center for Complimentary and Alternative Medicine also states that there is little evidence that bitter orange is any safer than ephedra.

GREEN TEA: BREWING MOSTLY HYPE

"Drink Away Your Weight?" This was the headline for a story on CBS's *The Early Show* in 2007. The story explored the increasing popularity of green tea and weight loss claims that went with it. Green tea is unlike most other herbal supplements. In its most common form, it can be found next to other teas and coffees in any grocery store. A person can buy teabags to brew at home, or get it ready-made in a bottle. In addition to its drinkable forms, substances made from green tea are available in capsules. Green tea is also the active ingredient in the

As researchers continue to study the health benefits of green tea, tests have shown it to be helpful in preventing or slowing the development of cancer, diabetes, and heart diseases. Yet, there is still no evidence that it plays a role in helping with weight loss, as some companies claim. Above, a woman picks green tea leaves in Hangzhou, China.

Metabolife "weight loss system," which involves taking two pills before each meal.

The National Center for Complimentary and Alternative Medicine lists several possible health benefits of green tea. The NCCAM and other medical organizations are currently studying these possible benefits. For example, green tea may have helpful effects against cancer, diabetes, and heart disease.

There is little data, however, that supports the idea that green tea can speed up weight loss. There may be some truth in advertisers' claims, but experts say that consumers are often not getting the full story. "In some cases the amount of a substance used in clinical studies that may have shown a slight change in weight or fat burning can be 5–20 times the amount in these beverages," clinical nutritionist Samantha Heller told *The Early Show*. Heller is an editor at *Health* magazine. "You would have to drink 10 bottles or more a day to get even close to those amounts."

Tea also contains caffeine, so anyone who is very sensitive to caffeine's effects (which may include jitteriness and upset stomach, or, in severe cases, seizure and irregular heart rhythms) should steer clear of green tea. The same is true for anyone taking drugs to prevent blood clotting, such as the drug warfarin. This is because small amounts of vitamin K in the tea can reduce the effectiveness of this kind of drug.

OTHER FAT BURNING CLAIMS

Samantha Heller may have said it best when she told *The Early Show* that food and supplement companies "like to throw around terms like 'thermogenesis.' " In fact, the word is used in ways—mainly in sales pitches—that are not accurate. What follows are a few other substances that claim to have thermogenic effects—or at least, something like them.

Pyruvate is a substance that occurs naturally in the body when the body digests **carbohydrates** and proteins. It's also found in red wine and in such foods as cheese and red apples. Some weight loss supplements contain pyruvate, whose root word means "fire." It's no wonder that people looking to burn fat are drawn to it. Unfortunately, in this case, there might not be much in a name. A few small studies have found a possible connection between pyruvate and slight weight loss, but those studies generally tested unreasonably large amounts of the substance. Pyruvate supplements also tend to be expensive, and are not worth the stomach upset and diarrhea they can possibly cause.

Chromium is a mineral found naturally in foods. It is an essential nutrient. It helps control blood sugar, and this makes it important in diabetes and heart disease research. Studies on chromium as a fat burner haven't shown that it actually burns fat. In general, studies have come up with no evidence, or have had mixed results. Furthermore, too much of the mineral can be toxic. (This is highly unlikely from food alone, but quite possible with supplements.) Users can suffer kidney, liver, muscle, and bone marrow damage from taking in too much chromium.

Guarana is a dried paste made from the seeds of a climbing shrub, a plant native to the Brazilian and Venezuelan rainforests. People in these regions consider guarana to have many health benefits and have long used it in beverages. The seeds contain caffeine—up to three times the amount in most coffee beans. This gives it a stimulant effect and causes a person to urinate more. Although some supplement manufacturers and consumers believe that guarana can lead to weight loss, there is little or no evidence to support this. However, guarana's stimulant effect can raise blood pressure, and cause

(continues on page 43)

Guarana grows naturally in Brazil and the Amazon rainforest. While some locals and supplement manufacturers believe use of the plant can help with weight loss, there is little to no evidence of this. In fact, use of guarana carries several health risks.

THE EPHEDRA BAN

Steve Bechler had his whole life ahead of him, and it promised to be a good one. At 23, he was an up-and-coming pitcher with the Baltimore Orioles. He and his wife, Kiley, were expecting a baby soon. Then one day, while training in Florida, Bechler collapsed on the playing field. The next day—February 17, 2003—he passed away.

According to medical reports, a number of factors played a part in Bechler's death from heatstroke. Bechler was slightly overweight, not eating properly, and not used to the hot weather in Florida. He was also regularly taking ephedra. Broward County medical examiner Dr. Joshua Perper reported finding "significant amounts" of the substance in his system at the time of his death, according to *USA Today.* "It is my professional opinion that the toxicity of ephedra played a significant role in the death of Mr. Bechler," Perper said to newspaper reporters, "although it's impossible to define mathematically the contribution of each one of the risk factors." CBS News reported that Bechler had taken three of the pills on an empty stomach the morning he collapsed.

Bechler's death is widely considered to be the final straw in an ongoing debate over the safety of ephedra. The drug was once commonly used (and heavily advertised) as a weight loss supplement. The FDA finally banned the ingredient altogether in the months following Bechler's death. But before that happened, the herb had been linked to several other deaths and additional cases of serious heart problems. In fact, it was already forbidden within the

(continues on page 42)

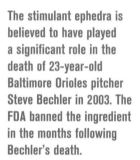

The stimulant ephedra is believed to have played a significant role in the death of 23-year-old Baltimore Orioles pitcher Steve Bechler in 2003. The FDA banned the ingredient in the months following Bechler's death.

(continued from page 41)

NFL, the Olympics, and the NCAA, as well as on military bases.

Bechler was reportedly taking an ephedra supplement called Xenadrine RFA-1. Even that supplement's maker, Cytodyne Technologies, admits that ephedra had long been on shaky ground before the young baseball player's death. "There was a storm brewing on ephedra all along," Bryan Glazer, president of the company that handles public relations for Cytodyne, told *The New York Times.* "The death of Steve Bechler turned a Category 1 storm into a Category 5 hurricane."

Even before the FDA's official ban, many supplement companies volunteered to pull their own ephedra-based products from shelves. They also scrambled to come up with a similar ingredient after news of Bechler's death. Newer, "ephedra-free!" supplements contain HCA, bitter orange, or other so-called thermogenic substances, often combined with each other.

(continued from page 39)

irregular heartbeat, dizziness, and anxiousness. Guarana may also cause prolonged bleeding and interact with blood-thinning medications.

Then there is HCA, a substance that comes from the Indian plant *garcinia cambogia*. HCA's full name is *hydroxycitric acid*. It is the main ingredient in the well-known diet pill Hydroxycut, which also contains green tea extract and other ingredients. Studies using animals have found that HCA may possibly help reduce body fat. Any evidence that it may lead to weight loss in humans is weak at best.

THE MYSTERY OF CLA (CONJUGATED LINOLEIC ACID)

CLA is a substance found naturally in meats, milk, and vegetable oils. It is in a class of its own among fat-burning supplements. It seems to sometimes result in fat loss, but exactly if and how it does this is poorly understood. According to the Web site of Wellness Partners, maker of the leading CLA brand Tonalin, the substance "decreases the amount of fat stored after eating, increases the rate of fat breakdown in fat cells, increases the rate of fat metabolism, and decreases the amount of fat cells."

The medical community doesn't share the company's certainty that CLA causes fat loss. The journal *Lipids in Health and Disease* published a report on treating weight gain caused by psychiatric drugs. The report suggested that CLA might help patients lose pounds that they gained because of taking certain medicines. But the report also noted that CLA's exact workings have yet to be proven.

At least two studies of CLA's effects on mice and rats resulted in bizarrely mixed findings that even suggest dangers to humans. Mice fed with CLA clearly lost weight, but they also grew excessive amounts of fat in their livers. In humans, excess fat in the liver is associated with *insulin resistance*. This is when the body's insulin, a hormone made by the pancreas, does not properly do its job of allowing the body to use blood sugar for energy. People with insulin resistance may develop type 2 diabetes. Rats, on the other hand, did not lose weight, but the CLA actually seemed to decrease the amount of fat in their livers.

At the least, researchers concluded, CLA could have significant effects on humans in terms of insulin resistance. According to head researcher Martha Belury, these mice and rats also show a range of possible side effects from taking CLA. "The question is, are humans more like mice or rats?" Belury asks. "We're probably somewhere in between."

CORTISOL: THE FAT HORMONE?

From bad moods to acne, **hormones** get the blame for a lot of things going on inside the human body.

KEEPING METABOLISM HEALTHY

When a person's body is going through the changes of puberty, it is especially important to treat it well. During adolescence, the body needs plenty of fuel for healthy growth and development. Check out these ideas for keeping your body running smoothly, and forget about trying a supplement.

1. Eat breakfast. Many people think they don't have time for breakfast, and will often skip it. Others think that skipping breakfast will help them lose weight (it won't). The truth is, breakfast really is "the most important meal of the day." Try to make time for it, even if it just means eating some fruit and toast on the way to the bus stop. Your body needs fuel first thing in the morning to help keep you running until lunchtime.

2. Just eat. Not eating enough in an attempt to lose weight can actually make you *gain* weight. This is because the human body is programmed to store a certain amount of energy. So, when you start skipping meals or eating very small amounts, your metabolism actually slows down. Eat when you're hungry and stop when you're satisfied, and your body will thank you.

3. Exercise. Getting **aerobic** exercise, such as running, biking, swimming, or playing a sport, is the best way to keep your heart and the rest of your body healthy. But not everyone likes the same kind of activities. If you don't like traditional sports, look around for something else that fits your tastes. Other activities could be yoga, dancing, Frisbee, or just playing outside. Muscle-building exercises,

(continues on page 46)

(continued from page 45)

such as lifting weights, can also help, since muscle burns far more calories than fat does.

4. Drink plenty of water. Plain, simple water has an amazing effect on the human body. It is one of the keys to keeping the body working properly, so be sure to drink several glasses per day.

One interesting theory within the weight loss industry is that hormones cause fat to gather around the abdomen. The companies that make Relacore, CortiSlim, and their competitors claim their products lower the body's levels of the hormone **cortisol.** This is the hormone that the body produces when a person is under stress.

Experts do suggest that too much cortisol may contribute to weight gain. They say that the hormone can cause a person to crave high-fat and high-calorie foods, which could lead to weight gain in some people. But diet pill companies make claims like this: "High levels of cortisol . . . can cause pound after pound to accumulate around your waist and tummy" (according to Relacore's Web site). There is simply no trustworthy scientific evidence to support that statement. Advertisers also try to make customers believe that their products will help melt away belly fat, but they aren't very clear about the exact way the product works. (The Web sites do point out that their products should be used in addition to diet and exercise.)

The connection between cortisol and weight gain is unclear and unproven—and so are the effects of any supplement.

Fat Blockers
and Carb Blockers

Another family of weight loss pills is the fat blockers. These medications and supplements are designed to "trap" the fat in foods. The companies that make fat blockers say that this stops the body from absorbing fat. A related type of supplement, the carb blocker, has also entered the scene. The companies that make these supplements claim that they do the same thing as fat blockers, only instead of fat, they block carbohydrates. As with other kinds of diet pills, these substances are usually not supported by reliable science.

ORLISTAT: THE FAT-BLOCKING DRUG

As already discussed, the prescription drug sibutramine (Meridia) is one FDA-approved appetite suppressant in stores today. The other approved weight loss medication, orlistat, is a *lipase inhibitor*—the scientific name for fat blocker. Lipase is a substance that breaks down fat in the digestive system. Lipase inhibitors attach themselves to some of the fat a person eats. That stops lipase from reaching the fat to digest it. Without lipase doing its job, the body cannot absorb fat. As a result, the fat exits the body as waste (through bowel movements).

In 1999, the FDA approved the first orlistat drug, Xenical (manufactured by Hoffman-LaRoche). The drug is available by prescription only. Doctors follow strict guidelines as to what kind of person can receive a prescription for Xenical, or any diet pill. People should not be given a prescription just because they want to lose a few pounds, the guidelines note. In 2006, the FDA approved a version of orlistat that people can buy without a prescription. The drug is called Alli, and is made by the drug company GlaxoSmithKline. The main difference between the two drugs is in how strong they are: One pill of Xenical is twice as strong as one pill of Alli. Both are to be taken three times a day.

Like any drug, orlistat has some drawbacks. For one thing, when the drug traps and carries fat out of the body, it may carry certain needed nutrients along with it. For this reason, patients taking orlistat are advised to take a multivitamin as well. Orlistat also has some *very* unpleasant effects. The drug has gained a lot of attention for its side effects, which can be downright embarrassing. Because of the extra fat traveling through the colon (lower intestines), a person taking this drug may experience:

- More frequent and often "oily" bowel movements
- Greater urgency in the need to have a bowel movement
- Increased flatulence (gas)

- Oily discharge from the rectum (passageway out of the body)
- Fecal incontinence—the inability to hold in a bowel movement, possibly leading to "accidents"

ORLISTAT GOES OVER THE COUNTER

With a rainbow-colored logo and a name that means "friend," Alli can seem to some people to be the answer to how to lose weight. In a history-making move in early 2007, the FDA approved this new version of the fat blocker orlistat. That approval made it the only weight loss medication available without a prescription. (The Alli label states that the drug is not recommended for use by anyone under 18.)

Drug company GlaxoSmithKline sold more than 2 million starter packages of Alli within four months of its introduction, earning huge amounts of money for the giant company. The company expects to sell more than $1.5 billion worth of the drug every year, which would make it a drug "blockbuster." That's a label that is almost always used for prescription drugs, according to the Prescription Access Litigation Project.

Alli is half as strong as Xenical, but it still produces the same nasty side effects—and only slightly less often than Xenical does. These can range from frequent gas to embarrassing "accidents" requiring a change of clothes.

It's the potential for these side effects that has some experts worried about possible abuse of the drug among some people—particularly those with eating disorders. Dr. Randall Flanery worries that the drug could be used as a

Orlistat generally results in some weight loss for people who meet the guidelines set for who can take the drug, *and* who are following a prescribed diet. According to a study described on Xenical's Web site, patients who dieted and took orlistat lost about twice as

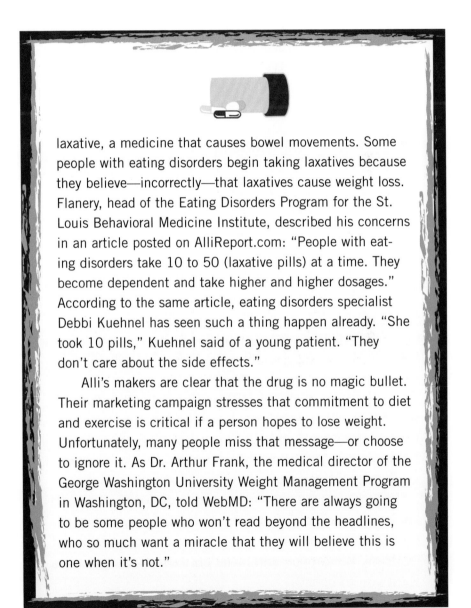

laxative, a medicine that causes bowel movements. Some people with eating disorders begin taking laxatives because they believe—incorrectly—that laxatives cause weight loss. Flanery, head of the Eating Disorders Program for the St. Louis Behavioral Medicine Institute, described his concerns in an article posted on AlliReport.com: "People with eating disorders take 10 to 50 (laxative pills) at a time. They become dependent and take higher and higher dosages." According to the same article, eating disorders specialist Debbi Kuehnel has seen such a thing happen already. "She took 10 pills," Kuehnel said of a young patient. "They don't care about the side effects."

Alli's makers are clear that the drug is no magic bullet. Their marketing campaign stresses that commitment to diet and exercise is critical if a person hopes to lose weight. Unfortunately, many people miss that message—or choose to ignore it. As Dr. Arthur Frank, the medical director of the George Washington University Weight Management Program in Washington, DC, told WebMD: "There are always going to be some people who won't read beyond the headlines, who so much want a miracle that they will believe this is one when it's not."

much weight as those who dieted without taking orlistat. However, the weight loss among the people who took the drug was modest—an average of 13.4 pounds after one year.

Some patients may decide that orlistat is just not worth the side effects. "Xenical is okay, but I experienced some embarrassing moments while on it," reads a posting on a Xenical discussion board on OB/GYN. net. "One being a day when I had to return home from work because an oily discharge began seeping from my bottom (yuck!)." Users are able to lessen their chances of embarrassing side effects by eating a low-fat diet, but the effects are still a worry for some.

CHITOSAN: NATURE'S ORLISTAT?

Chitosan comes from *chitin,* a substance that comes from the shells of lobsters, crabs, shrimp, and other shellfish. Supplement makers claim that when chitin is processed, the final product—chitosan—turns into a kind of fat magnet. This is a theory that may come from the longtime use of chitosan to purify dirty water for safe use by people. When chitosan is spread over water, oils and toxins rise up and cling to it. They can then be removed easily from the surface.

Chitosan is a type of **fiber**, a nutrient that is necessary for healthy digestion. It's different from common fiber that a person gets in his or her diet, such as that found in vegetables and whole grains. In theory, chitosan binds with fat, and that chitosan-bound fat becomes a kind of "grease ball" that is too large for the body to absorb. Instead, as with orlistat-bound fat, it leaves the body as waste matter. At least, this is what the makers of Chitosol, Fat Zapper, and other chitosan-based products want you to believe.

However, there is *very* little, if any, scientific evidence to support the claim that chitosan does any of that in the human body. Many studies, in fact, disprove it. For example, researchers at the Department of Nutrition and the Department of Internal Medicine at University of California, Davis, found that the effects of chitosan were not at all strong enough to cause weight loss. The researchers concluded that "the fat trapping claims associated with chitosan are unsubstantiated." In other words, it just doesn't work.

CARB BLOCKERS

Judging by the wild and ongoing popularity of low-carb foods and diets, it seems that many people now believe that it's carbohydrates—not fat—that cause weight gain. Carbohydrates, or carbs, are a common and important nutrient. Most carbs are found in foods that are made from plants. Some animal-based foods, such as milk, also contain carbs. Therefore, nearly all foods, from a bowl of broccoli to a candy bar, contain carbs.

Fruits, vegetables, and whole-grain breads and cereals contain carbohydrates. This is also true of cookies, cakes, and most other sweets, since both flour and sugar come from plants—flour from wheat, and sugar from sugar cane. Potatoes, beans, popcorn, and rice are other examples of foods with carbs.

An anti-carb craze hit the United States in the late 1990s, when many different diet books and even some doctors argued that eating a lot of carbohydrates caused weight gain. Part of the theory had to do with the way the body digests different types of sugars, which affects metabolism and feelings of hunger. It wasn't long before supplement companies got on board.

Diets low in carbohydrates have become increasingly popular, causing companies like Russell Stover to sell chocolate bars targeting people following low-carb regimens. Above are three types of Pecan Delights the company manufactured in 2003 to keep up with consumers' dietary concerns.

Enter the carb blockers: CarbSpa, CBlock, Accuslim, and countless other products claiming to prevent the digestion of carbs. The main ingredient in carb blockers (if they contain what they say) is usually phaseolamin, a substance that comes from white kidney beans. In theory, phaseolamin interferes with the body's ability to produce alpha-amylase, a substance that breaks down carbohydrates. When carbohydrates are broken down, they are turned into sugars that the body then uses for energy. Supplement companies claim that their carb blockers cause carbs to leave the body undigested instead of being used for energy or stored as fat for future energy needs.

It may come as no surprise that there is no scientific evidence that carb blockers do what they claim. There

THE PRICE OF FALSE
HEALTH CLAIMS

A note to supplement manufacturers, especially those selling weight loss products: Somebody's watching.

Some companies may think that they can get away with anything since they don't need the FDA's stamp of approval to sell their product. They're wrong. The Dietary Supplement Health and Education Act (DSHEA) of 1994 made it clear how the FDA is to control the supplement industry and check up on manufacturers' responsibilities. The manufacturer is responsible for checking that the product is safe, even though it doesn't need FDA approval to be sold. Companies must also show scientific evidence to back up any claims they make. Any company that violates the rules is informed of its violation(s) and ordered to make changes. Companies that still fail to follow the rules face serious penalties that include having the products taken away, and possible criminal charges.

The production and advertising of weight loss supplements have soared in recent years. While that has been happening, crackdowns on false claims have also soared. In 2004 alone, for example, the FDA sent warning letters to dozens of supplement companies whose Web sites were found to be making claims with no strong scientific support. The vast majority of the supplement products were fat and carb blockers.

Many supplement sellers make pretty much the same claims. Because of this, the Federal Trade Commission (FTC) came up with a list of claims that are automatically considered "red flags." The following are some claims that dishonest supplement makers advertise:

(continues on page 56)

(continued from page 55)

- Consumers who use the advertised product can lose two pounds or more per week (over four or more weeks) without reducing calorie intake and/ or increasing their physical activity.
- Consumers who use the advertised product can lose a lot of weight while still enjoying unlimited amounts of high-calorie foods.
- The advertised product will cause permanent weight loss, even when the user stops using the product.
- The advertised product will cause major weight loss by stopping the body from absorbing fat or calories.
- Consumers who use the advertised product (without medical supervision) can safely lose more than three pounds per week for a period of more than four weeks.
- Users can lose a lot of weight by wearing the advertised product on the body or by rubbing it into the skin.
- The advertised product will cause major weight loss for all users.
- Consumers who use the advertised product can lose weight only from those parts of the body where they wish to lose weight.

The claims themselves may use more exciting wording than this, but the idea is the same. In a 2004 testimony before the Committee on Governmental Affairs, FDA official

Robert E. Brackett gave some examples of actual statements made by supplement companies:

- "Eat All You Want! Block the Starch and Lose Weight!"
- "Neutralize up to 66 percent of the starch consumed in a meal."
- "Take 3 capsules before bedtime. Watch the fat disappear!"

Some of the companies that were warned have voluntarily taken back their statements or their products. Others have paid the price for refusing to follow the rules. Pinnacle Marketing, LLC, the maker of UltraCarb, agreed to pay more than $200,000 to settle federal charges. VisionTel Communications, advertisers of Chito-Trim and TurboTone, agreed to pay $750,000 after making false claims about these and several other products (including supplements advertised for purposes other than weight loss). In addition to these cases, the FDA has taken millions of dollars worth of products from manufacturers who have refused to correct themselves.

is no evidence that taking them will lead to weight loss. Melinda Safir, staff nutritionist with the Cooper Clinic in Dallas, told *Men's Fitness*: "The ability to choose what foods move from your plate into your mouth is the most powerful carbohydrate blocker and weight loss aid on the market. Every product promoted as a weight loss miracle pales in comparison to our own ability to control food selection and intake amount." The message is clear: The power to be healthy is yours and has nothing to do with the latest "miracle pill."

Taking the Focus Off the Scale

Many Americans are hearing the message that they need to lose weight. Some take this message too far, and try losing weight at all costs. One of these costs might be the person's own health. It's far better to focus on leading a healthy lifestyle than to worry about a number on the scale. This is especially true when a person is young and still growing.

THINK YOU NEED TO LOSE WEIGHT?

If you do, you're certainly not alone. Still, if you're under 18, there's a good chance that your view of yourself contradicts the medical reality. Despite the weight crisis among American children and teens, only about 15% are considered overweight or obese. If you are not among them, it's probably best to maintain your present weight (unless you are underweight). However, there are probably ways you could improve your habits. Most people, regardless of weight, could stand to eat better and be more physically active. Still, everyone should talk to a doctor before trying anything, including diet pills, a diet, or an exercise program.

When looking to become healthier, many people focus on numbers: body weight and BMI. But stepping on a scale at home cannot provide enough insight. Your BMI may not provide enough information either. Doctors often use BMI as a tool to get a picture of someone's overall health. But BMI only measures weight and height, not how much body fat you have, your family health history, whether you eat a healthy diet, or whether you exercise regularly.

It's important to see your doctor regularly. He or she can give you advice on ways to keep your body healthy and strong. Work with your doctor to set goals for new healthy behaviors. Then work on making these specific lifestyle changes. Your doctor (or a nutritionist, if your doctor recommends one) will ask you about your current habits, such as what and when you tend to eat, and how physically active you are each day. Together, you can target areas that could make you healthier and work on a plan for what you should do. It's good to check back with your doctor regularly to report on how you are doing.

Outside of the doctor's office, you are likely to hear talk of fat, carbs, protein, metabolism, and other buzzwords on television and in other media sources. It can be confusing. In general, burning more calories than you take in will result in weight loss. By the same logic, taking in more calories than you burn will result in weight gain. The way you "take in" calories is, of course, by eating food and drinking certain beverages. The way you burn calories is through physical activity and through

Some people have a warped view of their body, which can lead to anorexia and other eating disorders.

the everyday processes that go on inside your body. So, a balance of healthy eating and physical activity is the key to a healthy weight. A "healthy" weight is not the same for everyone. It is different for each person, so be careful not to look to your friends when deciding what is right for you.

It's important to remember that calories are not the big thing to think about when choosing a meal in your school cafeteria. Nutrition is what really matters when it comes to health. If you only paid attention to calories, you could end up lacking a lot of specific

FEEL THE BURN: HOW THE BODY USES ENERGY

All day long, your body uses up the calories in the food you eat—even when you're sleeping. Everything you do, whether it's running a marathon or typing a paper, uses up some energy. Body functions that you don't even think about—such as digestion and fighting disease—also need calories in order to happen. The chart below gives you an idea of how many calories you burn through some common physical activities.

MODERATE PHYSICAL ACTIVITY	APPROXIMATE CALORIES/HR FOR A 154-LB PERSON[a]
Hiking	370
Light gardening/yard work	330
Dancing	330
Golf (walking and carrying clubs)	330
Bicycling (<10 mph)	290
Walking (3.5 mph)	280
Weight lifting (general light workout)	220
Stretching	180

nutrients your body needs. For example, highly processed foods like candy and chips will have far fewer
vitamins, minerals, and other substances your body
needs. Whole grains, vegetables and fruits, and lean
protein will have more. It's okay to have candy and
chips sometimes, but if you want to fuel your body
well, it's best not to eat a lot of these kinds of things
every day. It's important to remember that the kinds of

VIGOROUS PHYSICAL ACTIVITY	APPROXIMATE CALORIES/HR FOR A 154-LB PERSON[a]
Running/jogging (5 mph)	590
Bicycling (>10 mph)	590
Swimming (slow freestyle laps)	510
Aerobics	480
Walking (4.5 mph)	460
Heavy yard work (chopping wood)	440
Weight lifting (vigorous effort)	440
Basketball (vigorous)	440

[a] Calories burned per hour will be higher for persons who weigh more than 154 lbs (70 kg) and lower for persons who weigh less.

Source: Adapted from *Dietary Guidelines for Americans 2005*, U.S. Departments of Agriculture and Health and Human Services.

foods you eat most often are part of what affect your overall health.

FOOD FOR THOUGHT

Let's take a closer look at food. It's important to try to get the most nutrition from your food choices. For some people, that can sound difficult, but it is easier than it sounds. Junk foods usually have more calories than more nutritious foods. Carbohydrates and protein have about 4 calories per gram, while fats (including saturated fats, unsaturated fats, trans fats, and cholesterol) have about twice that many. (Even though sugar is a carbohydrate, it tends to be hidden in foods, and its calories add up far more quickly than calories in healthier carbs.) So, for the same number of calories, you could eat either:

a) a complete meal of protein (such as chicken, fish, lean beef, or tofu) and healthy carbohydrates (such as vegetables and whole-grain rice), or

b) a candy bar.

Sure, choice "b" might sound more appealing at the moment, and it will certainly give you a burst of energy. But sugary foods like candy often don't stick with you for long. It's likely that you would be hungry again in no time at all. You also would have eaten few of the nutrients your body needs. That doesn't mean people should *never* eat candy, but it does mean candy should not make up a big part of a person's meals and snacks. Think about this when you reach for a snack: You could grab a few cookies, chips, or crackers, or you could enjoy fruit or raw vegetables and a scoop of a low-fat dairy product (such as low-fat yogurt or cottage cheese). Every food has a place in a balanced, varied diet. Still, it's best to reach most often for the foods that provide the most of what your body needs.

Many schools are now offering healthier lunch and snack options for students, including machines stocked with water and juice rather than soda.

Here are some other healthy ideas to think about when making food choices:

- Choose a side salad instead of fries when you get a sandwich. Salad has many more nutrients and will fill you up and keep you going.
- Try using regular olive oil plus red wine vinegar or lemon juice on your salads instead of thick, creamy salad dressing. Many packaged dressings have ingredients that come from a laboratory, not a garden.

- Try using mustard or another spread such as hummus on a sandwich instead of mayonnaise.
- Try low-fat cottage cheese and plain yogurt instead of whole-milk dairy products. If you want some flavor in your yogurt, mix it up with your favorite fruit and some honey.
- Instead of chips, snack on raisins, sliced apples, baby carrots, or a few rice-cake chips with your sandwich.
- Choose healthier drinks: Sodas and sports drinks provide far fewer nutrients than beverages such as milk and fresh fruit and vegetable juices. Diet sodas may seem like a healthy choice because they are low in calories, but they also have added salt and certain ingredients your body just does not need. Plus, believe it or not, many juices are no healthier than sodas. Look for juice that says "100% juice" on its label. (In addition to other beverage choices, remember to drink a lot of water!)

Sometimes, people find that even when they reach for healthy foods, they eat more than they wanted without realizing it. Even a very nutritious meal can cause a person to feel the way he or she does after a huge Thanksgiving dinner. This is especially true when going out to eat at a restaurant. Today's portions are nearly twice as big as what they were 20 years ago. Fast-food places have "supersized," other restaurants are piling more on plates, and prepackaged snacks generally contain much more than one serving. These trends can lead to overeating, often without the person realizing it until he or she is uncomfortably full. Eating while being distracted by something else, such as TV, adds to the problem. Try these tips to help stay aware of the signals your body sends you when you're full:

- Don't eat foods directly out of the bag or box. Put the amount you want in a dish or on a plate, and put the package away. If you want more, you can always go back and get some.
- When you go out to eat, pay attention throughout the meal to how full you are getting. You don't have to eat everything on your plate all at once. Ask for a doggy bag to take the rest home if you're full but want to save it for later. Splitting a meal with a friend is another idea.
- Don't eat in front of the TV. This can make you eat without thinking about how hungry you are, and before you know it, you've eaten far more than you want. Sit at a table and actually enjoy your food.
- Don't "supersize" fast foods, and don't make fast foods a big part of your diet. They're usually not very healthy, and often don't even taste very good compared with more nutritious foods.
- Eat breakfast. This one bears repeating. "[Many overweight people] get up in the morning and say 'I'm going to start my diet today,' and they eat little or no breakfast and a light lunch," Dr. Rena Wing, a psychiatry professor and co-developer of a research study known as the National Weight Control Registry, told *FDA Consumer.* "Then they get hungry and

consume most of their calories late in the day. Successful weight losers have managed to change this pattern."

PUTTING YOUR FUEL TO USE

A healthy diet is not enough if you want to be as healthy as you can be. Exercise is key to keeping your body strong and full of energy. Experts recommend that everyone get moderate to vigorous physical activity every day, or on as many days as possible. Examples of moderate activity include gentle walking, bicycling around your neigh-borhood, dancing, and stretching. "Vigorous" would apply to anything that really works up a sweat. This can include activities like running, brisk walking, or playing basketball. These are just some basic examples. The key is to find something you enjoy. Here are some other tips to help get you moving:

- Start off slow. Don't wake up and run five miles if you've never done it in your life. This would not only exhaust and discourage you, but it could be dangerous. Just make an effort to do some exercise every day.
- Break it up. According to *FDA Consumer* magazine, some studies show that several short sessions of exercise can be as helpful to your body as one long one. If you don't have a free hour to get in your daily exercise all at once, try fitting in a few shorter sessions of activities you enjoy. This might mean stretching when you get up in the morning and riding bikes with friends after school.
- Grab it when you can. You might be surprised at how many hidden fitness opportunities a

In addition to a healthy diet, exercise is vital to keeping your body strong and full of energy. Above, Ivonne Borrero and her 11-year-old son, Jose Roman, walk along Boston Harbor in 2007 as part of a federal program to combat childhood obesity, called "We Can!" It encourages subtle changes at home to help kids learn healthy habits.

typical day holds. Has your mom been after you to do some yard work? That's vigorous physical activity right there. Do you usually catch a ride to school? Try walking or riding your bike, if the distance is reasonable and the route is safe. Maybe the best advice of all is to choose physical activity over "screen time." If you're bored, resist the urge to sit down at the computer or in front of the TV. Instead, turn on your stereo and dance around the room. Or go outside, and do just about anything.

- Recruit a friend. When it comes to exercise, nothing makes the activity more fun than having a partner. Ask a friend to join a swimming or exercise class with you at the local YMCA or recreation center. Plan a daily walk or run together after school, or on Saturday mornings. Consider taking up a team sport—that way, you'll have guaranteed company every time. Remember, school isn't the only place that offers sports. See what's available through your community's recreation department.

MEDICAL INTERVENTIONS

For some people, lifestyle changes may not be enough to get to a weight that medical experts consider healthy. Some obese people therefore choose major medical treatments in order to lose a significant amount of weight.

As previously discussed, two weight loss medications are currently available by prescription. Sibutramine (Meridia), which suppresses appetite, is approved for use in obese patients age 16 or older. Orlistat (Xenical), a fat blocker, is approved for children 12 and older and adults. Candidates for these medications are not simply people who want to lose a few pounds, even if their doctors tell them they should lose weight. A patient must be severely overweight and meet certain other criteria before a doctor will consider prescribing medication.

If all else—including diet, exercise, and medication combined—seems to fail, surgery is one more option available to some very obese people. Bariatric surgeries make changes to the digestive system so that less food can comfortably be eaten and/or fewer calories can be absorbed. (These surgeries are extremely rare for teens and performed mainly on very obese adults.) Gastric bypass surgery, the most common bariatric procedure performed today, has two parts:

- A small pouch is created in the upper part of the stomach so that a person can only eat the small amount of food that the pouch can hold in one sitting. This decreases the total amount of food a person can eat.
- A piece of the intestine is attached to the pouch, causing food to literally bypass (skip) the rest of the stomach and other parts of the digestive system. This reduces the amount of calories and nutrients the body absorbs.

Gastric bypass surgeries, like any type of major surgery, carry serious risks. Patients may experience digestive problems for weeks or more following the procedure. Further, patients considering gastric bypass must be ready to make a lifelong commitment to major diet changes, including sticking to a strict new diet and taking daily nutritional supplements.

The question of whether gastric bypass surgery is appropriate for teens is very controversial. Adapting to life after the procedure is challenging enough for adults, who are not dealing with issues of physical and emotional development in addition to such a dramatic event. For this reason, the criteria for being elegible for gastric bypass surgery are even stricter for adolescents than for adults. In general, a teen must:

- have a BMI of 40 or higher
- have tried unsuccessfully to lose weight for at least 6 months

- have already stopped growing taller
- have serious health problems related to weight (such as type 2 diabetes)

OTHER PLAYERS IN THE WEIGHT LOSS INDUSTRY

Weight loss supplements, whether in the form of pills, powders, foods, or drinks, are a booming business. However, there are many other ways in which companies claim to help people achieve the weight, body shape, and overall look of their dreams. Here are some examples of other weight loss programs and claims:

- **Diet programs.** The word *diet* can mean many things. Literally, *diet* means the way you choose to eat, but many people use the word *diet* to mean a way to eat to lose weight. If you're convinced you need to follow a certain program in order to lose weight, think again. For one thing, no **fad diet** (such as one that severely restricts carbs) has proven to be the weight loss answer, and is especially not the way to be healthy. Furthermore, following any program, even one that encourages a variety of foods, often means paying membership fees, buying books and the company's own foods, and sometimes other expenses.
- **Exercise equipment.** There's certainly nothing wrong with working out. On the contrary, any kind of exercise is a good thing. Commercials or infomercials that are trying to sell some new

- undergo a psychological evaluation to check that he or she is ready for the necessary lifestyle changes.

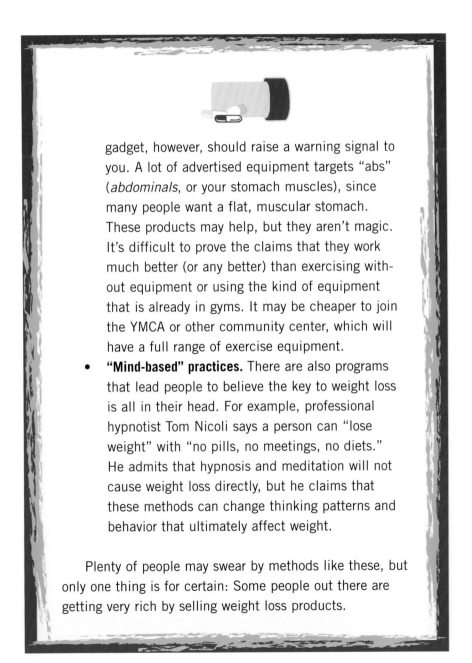

gadget, however, should raise a warning signal to you. A lot of advertised equipment targets "abs" (*abdominals*, or your stomach muscles), since many people want a flat, muscular stomach. These products may help, but they aren't magic. It's difficult to prove the claims that they work much better (or any better) than exercising without equipment or using the kind of equipment that is already in gyms. It may be cheaper to join the YMCA or other community center, which will have a full range of exercise equipment.

- **"Mind-based" practices.** There are also programs that lead people to believe the key to weight loss is all in their head. For example, professional hypnotist Tom Nicoli says a person can "lose weight" with "no pills, no meetings, no diets." He admits that hypnosis and meditation will not cause weight loss directly, but he claims that these methods can change thinking patterns and behavior that ultimately affect weight.

Plenty of people may swear by methods like these, but only one thing is for certain: Some people out there are getting very rich by selling weight loss products.

Choosing to have any bariatric surgery is a major, life-altering decision. It's important to remember that the vast majority of teens, even those who are very overweight, can be healthy without surgery.

FINDING SUPPORT

Committing to a healthier lifestyle and sticking to it is not always easy. That's why it's best to involve your family in your goals of eating healthier and getting more exercise. You're going to need to tell whomever does the food shopping in your family if you want to try a funny-looking tropical fruit or a new kind of whole-grain cereal. You might even inspire your family members to try new foods and recipes, and to spend time together doing fun physical activities. You can also let your friends know about your new goals. Good friends will respect your healthy new habits, and maybe even join you in some of them.

Boosting Body Image, Saving Self-Esteem

Millions of Americans are not happy with their weight. A good number of them are teens. One 2001 survey found that 60% of middle and high school students worry about being too fat or too thin. Another survey in 2005 found that only "slightly more than half" of boys and "a little more than a third" of girls are happy with their bodies. Some boys may be concerned that their muscles aren't big enough. Other boys with body concerns and the majority of girls with body concerns believe they are too fat.

HOW TEENS FEEL
"Ugh i hate my body i dont like the way my stomach bulges out when i sit!!!!!!!!! . . . my bf . . . loves the way i

look & he accepts me for who i am but, why can't i do the same??"

"i feel fat ALL THE TIME and just so unhappy with my body."

"I still hate my body and think that i should be way smaller . . . i feel huge . . . yet one of my friends is like, 'you have no fat on you . . . so what are you obsessing about?'"

"I know that I'm not 'overweight' but I FEEL like I am and can't look at myself."

These are excerpts from postings found on teen chat sites. Could they just as easily be from a conversation you and a friend had this week? Body image—the way you feel about your physical appearance—can be a powerful influence on your self-esteem, or the way you feel about yourself overall. The reverse is also true: For some young people, low self-esteem causes them to develop hatred for their bodies. Unfortunately, more teens seem to have a negative body image than a positive one.

Teen bodies go through major changes due to puberty, which can cause a lot of concern about appearance. Many young people put on weight before a growth spurt occurs, and that can make them feel that they are "too fat." A greater focus on fashion, relationships, and the media also contributes to young people's concern with their looks.

At a time when teens are figuring out who they really are, the slightest incident or comment can have a huge impact. That impact might cause a teen's body image and self-esteem to come crashing down. For example, a grandmother who calls her granddaughter "big-boned" like herself could unknowingly make the girl decide she is just plain "big." A not-so-innocent remark, such as one from a classmate in a mean mood, can be flat-out devastating.

As illustrated in the excerpts given here, a lot of body image problems revolve around weight, in particular. Many girls see themselves as "fat," even when others around them clearly disagree. The girl whose "bf" likes her as she is, and the one whose friend can't understand what she's "obsessing about," are examples of how some girls see their bodies in untrue ways. Many teens look to the media to get an ideal of what's attractive, or even just normal. They may believe that the images they see on TV, in movies, and in magazines are looks they should copy. This, experts say, is where much of the trouble starts.

AS SEEN ON TV

If you had to choose words to describe a famous supermodel, your description would definitely include "skinny." If you were to flip through *People* magazine's annual "Hottest Bachelors" issue, you would see guys whom you could describe as "chiseled," "buff," or "built."

People (especially young people) have long admired the looks of certain celebrities or advertising models. In today's media, unfortunately, it is almost always just the thin women and muscular men who are shown as attractive. But looking like the people you see in the media is extremely unrealistic. It's even more unrealistic now than it was when your parents were teenagers. According to the Social Issues Research Centre in the United Kingdom, the weight of an average advertising model is 23% lower than that of an average woman. Twenty years ago, the difference was only 8%. The organization also found that less than 5% of women naturally have the kind of body portrayed in advertising. A key word here is "naturally." In many cases, female

Many celebrities work hard to look fit. Actress Jessica Biel is well known for her never-too-thin, toned figure. Along with a healthy diet, her trainer, Jason Walsh, told *People* in 2007 that he helps the actress commit to a rigorous hour-long workout three to five times a week that includes a half-mile jog along with two 200-meter, 150-meter, and 100-meter sprints.

celebrities do very unnatural things in order to achieve a thin body. Male celebrities will also often go to extremes to get as muscular as they are.

There have been many studies examining the relationship between media images and young people's body images. The message from these findings is clear: The more media you consume (for example, the more TV you watch or the more celebrity magazines you read), the more you will search your own body for what you think may be "flaws." If you tend to surround yourself with a lot of media images, it's important to keep in mind that the people shown are *not* examples of how you should look, or how people in real life look. Think about it. Celebrities have access to:

- Personal trainers
- Personal chefs and personalized nutrition programs
- Top makeup and wardrobe crews
- Cosmetic surgery or similar treatments (which, regardless of cost, are never a good idea for young people)

In the case of images in magazines, photos are changed on computers to erase any wrinkles, zits, scars, or similar things on a person's skin. That is why all the photos you see of people in magazines show them with extremely smooth skin—almost like plastic. Computer programs can also make a person in a photo look much thinner than he or she does in real life.

Thus, as carefree as some of these people may appear, their looks take work—sometimes unrealistic and unreasonable amounts of it. Slowly, some celebrities are finally saying enough is enough. Supermodel Tyra Banks

(continues on page 82)

Model/TV host Tyra Banks embraced her curves after giving up the strict diet of a supermodel and putting on some weight. In 2007, Banks happily posed in a bathing suit alongside a paparazzi shot of herself that caused the media to call her "fat."

HOLLYWOOD'S WEIGHT GAME

If you look at the widely published snapshots of their daily lives, Hollywood stars may seem not to have a care in the world. The fact is there's at least one care that's likely on the minds of many celebrities. There is an unspoken message they receive every day: Stay thin, or suffer public humiliation.

Today, tabloids watch celebrities' weight like investors watch the stock market. A star's recent weight loss or gain can easily push all other news out of the way, making for a popular cover story. Beaches seem to be a particularly favorite hangout for photographers. Tabloid readers can find photos of celebrities sunbathing or out on boats in nearly any issue. The captions are usually favorable—for example, talking about a celebrity "showing off her bikini-worthy bod"—but attention is still being focused on the person's weight. "As a culture, we're all sort of obsessed with our weight," said Ken Baker of *Us Weekly* in a 2005 interview with CNN. "We're obsessed with celebrities, so of course we're going to be obsessed with celebrities' weight."

As stars work to stay thin (whether through healthy or unhealthy means), many seem to face a no-win situation. They find themselves walking a fine line between being thin and "scary skinny." Several women in Hollywood, including Jamie-Lynn Sigler, Mary-Kate Olsen, Katherine McPhee, and Paula Abdul, have gone public with their struggles with eating disorders.

Other thin celebrities face rumors that they have eating disorders, even though they have said loudly and firmly

(continues on page 82)

(continued from page 81)

that they don't. Keira Knightley and Kate Hudson, for example, each filed lawsuits when tabloids claimed that they suffered from eating disorders. "There are plenty of stars who are going after the tabloids right now," Harvey Levin, attorney and managing editor of the entertainment Web site TMZ. com, told CNN. "And this does not have anything nearly to do with money as it does (with) making a point to them that, 'Yes, you know what? I may be fair game, but I'm only fair game when it comes to telling the truth.' "

The most damaging aspect of celebrity weight hype, experts say, may be its effect on the young public. "It's a terrible message to young women who idolize these people," Lynn Grefe of the National Eating Disorders Association told CNN. "These Hollywood people are role models . . . we went after baseball players for drug use. We should be having hearings on Hollywood for . . . the message they're sending (because they are) sending kids into these terrible, potentially life-threatening illnesses."

(continued from page 79)

is one person who allowed herself to live normally after years of being a very thin fashion model. She stopped eating such a strict diet, which resulted in some weight gain. Pictures were taken of her on vacation that caused many cruel people to make fun of her for being "fat." She admits that those comments bothered her, but she told the entertainment show *ExtraTV* that she hopes the event will have a positive effect on youth. "Young girls talk about how much they hate themselves, and how . . . when they look at me, they feel more beautiful because I'm curvy, and it's okay," Banks said.

BODY IMAGE AND HEALTH

An eating disorder is a negative body image spun out of control, and it can be life-threatening. Eating disorders are caused and made worse by a variety of factors, including media images, messages from family or peers, and low self-esteem.

The two most common eating disorders are anorexia nervosa and bulimia. A person suffering from anorexia nervosa (often called simply "anorexia") eats so little that the person causes serious damage to his or her health. With bulimia, a person binges (eats a large amount of food in a short time) and purges (tries to gets rid of the food he or she has eaten by vomiting, taking laxatives, or exercising excessively). The National Eating Disorders Association estimates that around 10 million females and 1 million males in the United States suffer from an eating disorder. Eating disorders are medical conditions that have complex emotional, social, and biological causes. They often begin with a negative body image and thinking too much about weight. A person with an eating disorder may become so obsessed that no matter how much weight is lost, he or she still sees nothing but "fat."

Sometimes people with eating disorders abuse diet pills as part of their weight-control efforts. In search of a "quick fix," sufferers may also abuse substances like the following, which can have dangerous results:

Laxatives. These are drugs or supplements meant for the treatment of constipation (inability to produce regular bowel movements). The abuse of laxatives—that is, taking many of them, taking them too often, and/or taking them for the wrong reasons—causes diarrhea. People might think they are losing calories and weight this way, but all they are really losing is a lot of fluids. This is dangerous because the human body needs fluids to work properly. Dehydration (extreme fluid loss) and electrolyte imbalances (a related problem) can severely damage the heart, and even lead to a heart attack.

Diuretics. These drugs cause the body to flush out fluids through urine. People who abuse diuretics for weight control may think losing water will mean losing weight. Like laxative abuse, however, this is both ineffective and dangerous.

Ipecac Syrup. This age-old medication for causing vomiting can be extremely dangerous. It is meant only for cases of accidental poisoning or drug overdose, and even then, it should never be taken without a doctor's okay. Taking this substance incorrectly can cause muscle weakness or stiffness, seizures, shock, or even death from breathing in vomited material. At the very least, the effects are nasty—and they won't cause weight loss.

Eating disorders, and the drug abuse that often goes with them, are serious problems. Treatment is needed to help get the person back to being healthy and happy. If you, a friend, or a loved one has an eating disorder—or even if you *think* you or someone you love has one—get help right away. You can start by talking to a parent or other trusted adult, such as a coach or school counselor. You can also contact:

- The National Eating Disorders Association, or NEDA (www.nationaleatingdisorders.org or 1–800–931–2237). This is the nation's largest

Even models suffer from worries about body image, and make
unhealthy choices as a result. Brazilian model Ana Carolina
Reston, shown here modeling in 2005, died in 2006 at age
21 from anorexia-related causes.

ARE YOU IN DANGER?

Many young people are not thrilled with their bodies, or with themselves overall. These feelings are often mild and temporary, and do improve. For some, though, negative body image and poor self-esteem may become serious health hazards. Seek help if you or a friend:

- Seem very worried about the fat, calorie, or carb content in foods
- Seem to eat very little
- Have unusual eating rituals, such as shifting food around the plate or taking carefully measured bites
- Seem to fear eating and the idea of gaining any weight
- Have lost a lot of weight in a short amount of time
- Seem to exercise excessively
- Have a habit of going to the bathroom right after meals
- Use or have talked about using diet pills, laxatives, or similar products
- Go to Web sites that promote unhealthy weight loss methods or eating disorders
- Make mean comments about own appearance
- Seem depressed, moody, or constantly tired

These signs, individually, do not necessarily mean you or a friend have an eating disorder. But they are worth discussing with a trusted adult or someone at the organizations listed in this chapter. You could be helping to save a life.

non-profit organization dedicated to eating disorders awareness, treatment, and support.

- Something Fishy (www.something-fishy.org/ treatmentfinder/ or 1–866–690–7239). This organization's site can connect you to a variety of treatment and support options in your area.
- EDReferral.com (www.edreferral.com). This is a leading online database for eating disorders treatment, support, and information.

LOVE YOUR BODY, LOVE YOURSELF

Although it may not happen overnight, you can learn to appreciate and be content with the person you are and the package you came in. That's not to say that you can't ever change anything about how you look. For example, if you think a drastic new hairstyle or color would be fun, go for it—after careful consideration and talking to your parents, of course. But remember that there is no one rule of what is beautiful. Deciding that you are happy with the way you look is a positive step toward really liking yourself—and being truly happy. Here's a summary of expert advice on the matter:

- **Spare yourself the images.** Immersing yourself in fashion and celebrity gossip magazines can result in losing some self-esteem. You are doing yourself a favor by steering clear of these. Consider picking out a good book instead.
- **Avoid the scale.** It's too easy to let your body image and self-esteem rest on a number. There are many important measures for how good a person is, but weight is not one of them.
- **Dress comfortably.** It's that number thing again. Trying to squeeze into a size that is

American Idol contestant-turned-Oscar winner Jennifer Hudson promotes a healthy body image at any size. Above, the *Dreamgirls* star—who won the Best Supporting Actress Oscar for her role in the film in 2007—waves on the red carpet at the 2008 Academy Awards.

too small will only make you physically uncomfortable. Also, because too-small clothing won't flatter your body, you're also likely to feel discouraged by what you see in the mirror. The same goes for styles themselves. If you want to follow celebrity fashion or try out a new trend, pick the size that fits you best.

- **List what you like about yourself.** What positive traits do you see in yourself? Everyone has them—don't be shy. Do you tend to make people laugh? Do you have a knack for drawing? Maybe you're a good listener, the one all your friends come to for advice. Write this stuff down. Post the list where you can see it every day, or keep it in a private place and refer to it when you feel yourself having doubts.

- **Banish negative thoughts.** Pay attention to your inner self-talk. When you hear a put-down about yourself, stop it in its tracks. Refer to your "positive traits" list, or call a friend who makes you feel good about yourself.

It may sound simple, but it's true: Happiness starts with taking care of your physical and mental health. Using diet pills or any other unhealthy weight loss method does exactly the opposite. The most important step people can take in becoming healthier is to become happy with who they are right now.

CHRONOLOGY

1930s   The first weight loss drug, containing a chemical called dinitrophenol (DNP), is developed. It causes people to "sweat out" food energy rather than storing it. DNP is quickly pulled from the market after causing medical problems, and even death, by "overheating" the body.

1950s   Amphetamines, or stimulant drugs, become popular as diet pills. Serious side effects and withdrawal symptoms cause its popularity to fade. Approval for weight loss use is eventually reversed.

1976   The OTC appetite suppressant Dexatrim is introduced. Its success and popularity last more than two decades.

1992   A pharmacy journal reports the work of the University of Rochester's Dr. Michael Weintraub, who has discovered that the combination of fenfluramine and phentermine is effective for weight loss. The fen-phen craze begins.

1996   The Mayo Clinic reports serious heart problems in a high percentage of fen-phen users.

1997   Fen-phen and a related drug, Redux, are pulled from the market.

1997   The FDA approves the prescription appetite suppressant sibutramine (brand name Meridia), the first prescription weight loss drug of its kind.

1999   The FDA approves orlistat (brand name Xenical), the first-ever prescription fat blocker.

2000   The Yale University School of Medicine finds that phenylpropanolamine (PPA), the active ingredient in Dexatrim, increases the risk of hemorrhagic stroke. The FDA advises drug companies to remove the ingredient from all of their products.

February 2003 The stimulant ephedra, widely used for weight loss, contributes to the death of Orioles pitcher Steve Bechler.

December 2003 The FDA officially takes ephedra off the market.

2007 The FDA approves Alli, an OTC version of orlistat. It is the first-ever approved OTC weight loss drug of its kind, and the only approved OTC diet pill.

GLOSSARY

Calorie   Unit of energy value in food

Carbohydrate   A compound of carbon, hydrogen, and oxygen, formed mostly by green plants. Most foods contain carbohydrates.

Cortisol   A hormone involved in metabolism. Cortisol levels may rise under physical or emotional stress, and high cortisol levels increase blood pressure and blood sugar levels.

Ephedra   An extract of the eastern Asian plant ma huang, containing ephedrine

Fad diet   Any currently popular diet, usually not condoned by the medical community

Fiber   Indigestible matter found in plant foods that helps move food through the intestines.

Hormone   A substance circulating in body fluids that causes a specific type of activity within cells

Metabolism   The process by which bodies change the "fuel" we eat into the energy we need to breathe, digest, and carry out other life functions

Over-the-counter (OTC)   Describing a medication that is available without a prescription

Placebo   A "fake" (inactive) substance given for the purpose of comparison with the effects of a real medication. Placebos are most often used in scientific studies of new medications.

Side effect   Any effect of a medication other than its desired effects

(Dietary) Supplement   A product containing one or more ingredients meant to have an effect on health. Dietary supplements are considered neither foods nor medications.

Suppress   To prevent by keeping down or lowering the value of something

Thermogenesis   The production of heat in the body

BIBLIOGRAPHY

"Advisory Letter to Dietary Supplement Distributors about Unsubstantiated Weight Loss Claims." U.S. Food and Drug Administration, October 22, 2004. Available online. URL: www.cfsan.fda.gov/~dms/wl-ltr17.html. Accessed August 23, 2007.

"American Heart Association Guidelines for Selecting a Weight Loss & Maintenance Program." American Heart Association, 2007. Available online. URL: www.americanheart.org/presenter.jhtml?identifier=2884. Accessed August 23, 2007.

"Australia: New Research Shows that Smoking Increases Weight Gain." Medical News Today, October 24, 2007. Originally obtained from ASH, Action on Smoking and Health, United Kingdom. Available online. URL: www.medicalnewstoday.com/articles/86425.php. Accessed November 13, 2007.

Bodley, Hal. "Medical examiner: Ephedra a factor in Bechler death." *USA Today*, March 13, 2003. Available online. URL: www.usatoday.com/sports/baseball/al/orioles/2003–03–13-bechler-exam_x.htm. Accessed October 30, 2007.

Brackett, Robert. "Dietary Supplement Safety Act: How is FDA Doing After 10 Years? (Testimony)." U.S. Department of Health and Human Services, June 8, 2004. Available online. URL: www.hhs.gov/asl/testify/t040608b.html. Accessed November 13, 2007.

Bren, Linda. "Losing Weight: Start By Counting Calories." *FDA Consumer Magazine*, January-February 2002. Available online. URL: www.fda.gov/FDAC/features/2002/102_fat.html. Accessed November 13, 2007.

Brody, Jane E. "Weight-Loss Drugs: Hoopla and Hype." *The New York Times*, April 24, 2007. Available online. URL: www.nytimes.com. Accessed August 23, 2007.

"Carb blockers for fat loss. Ask Our Experts: composition and effectiveness of weight-loss supplements." *Men's Fitness*, August 2003. Available online. URL: http://findarticles.com/p/articles/mi_m1608/is_8_19/ai_105853422. Accessed November 13, 2007.

Carroll, Shawna L., Rebecca E. Lee, Harsohena Kaur, Kari J. Harris, Myra L. Strother, and Terry T.-K. Huang. "Smoking, Weight Loss Intention and Obesity-Promoting Behaviors in College Students." *Journal of the American College of Nutrition* 25 no. 4 (2006): 348–353. Available online. URL: www.jacn.org/cgi/content/abstract/25/4/348. Accessed November 13, 2007.

"Childhood Overweight." The Endocrine Society and the Hormone Foundation. Available online. URL: www.obesityinamerica.org/childhoodoverweight.html. Accessed August 27, 2007.

"CLA and Weight Loss." WellnessPartners.com. Available online. URL: www.wellnesspartners.com/tonalin/weight-loss.html. Accessed November 13, 2007.

Cohen, Kate. "Fen Phen Nation." Frontline (PBS), November 13, 2003. Available online. URL: www.pbs.org/wgbh/pages/frontline/shows/prescription/hazard/fenphen.html. Accessed October 30, 2007.

"Conjugated Linoleic Acid (CLA)." IronMagazine.com, September 6, 2002. Available online. URL: www.ironmagazine.com/review9.html. Accessed November 13, 2007.

Croatto, Pete. "A Weight-y Matter." Natural Products Insider, October 16, 2007. Available online. URL: www.naturalproductsinsider.com/articles/a-weight-y-matter.html. Accessed November 13, 2007.

Dahl, Melissa. "Diet pill's icky side effects keep users honest." MSNBC, July 6, 2007. Available online. URL: www.msnbc.msn.com/id/19587389. Accessed October 30, 2007.

"Diet Forums: Health & Support." Calorie Count from About.com. Available online. URL: www.calorie-count.com/forums/post/32743.html. Accessed November 13, 2007.

"Diet Pills, Laxatives and Dangerous Methods." Something Fishy, 2007. Available online. URL: www.something-fishy.org/dangers/methods.php. Accsesed November 13, 2007.

"Diet Pills: Too Good to Be True?" iVillage.com. Available online. URL: www.kndu.com/Global/story.asp?S=5201181. Accessed November 13, 2007.

Donnelly, Kathleen. "Diet Pills: A Dubious History." MSN Health & Fitness, 2007. Available online. URL: http://health.msn.com/fitness/articlepage.aspx?cp-documentid=100148215. Accessed August 28, 2007.

"Drink Away Your Weight?" The Early Show (CBS News), April 28, 2007. Available online. URL: www.cbsnews.com/stories/2007/04/27/earlyshow/saturday/main2737502.shtml. Accessed November 13, 2007.

"Drug Name: Xenical/Orlistat Capsules." Thomson Center-Watch (Clinical Trials Listing System) Patient Resources, June 29, 2004. Available online. URL: www.centerwatch.com/patient/drugs/dru566.html. Accessed January 2, 2008.

"Eating disorders warning signs." ANRED (Anorexia and Related Eating Disorders), February 27, 2006. Available online. URL: www.anred.com/warn.html. Accessed November 29, 2007.

"Eating Disorders: Body Image and Advertising." HealthyPlace.com, April 25, 2000. Available online. URL: www.healthyplace.com/communities/Eating_Disorders/body_image_advertising.asp. Accessed August 28, 2007.

"Fact Sheet: Advertising and Health." National Organization for Women (NOW) Foundation, a campaign of the Women's Health Project, 2007. Available online. URL: http://loveyourbody.nowfoundation.org/factsheet.html. Accessed November 13, 2007.

"FDA panel approves over-the-counter diet pill." MSNBC, January 24, 2006. Available online. URL: www.msnbc.msn.com/id/10987529. Accessed November 13, 2007.

Fritch, Jamie. "Chitosan: Revolutionizing Weight Loss?" Vanderbilt University, Psychology Department. Available online. URL: www.vanderbilt.edu/AnS/psychology/health_psychology/chitosan.htm. Accessed November 13, 2007.

Gades, Matthew D., and Judith S. Stern. "Chitosan Supplementation and Fecal Fat Excretion in Men." *Obesity Research* 11 (2003): 683–688. Available online. URL: www.obesityresearch.org/cgi/content/abstract/11/5/683. Accessed November 13, 2007.

"Gastrointestinal Surgery for Severe Obesity." Weight Control Information Network, a service of the National Institute of Diabetes and Digestive and Kidney Diseases, December 2004. NIH Publication No. 04–4006. Available online. URL: http://win.niddk.nih.gov/publications/gastric.htm#issurgfor. Accessed January 3, 2008.

"Glaxo sells 2 million alli kits—projects $1.5 billion in annual sales." Prescription Access Litigation, October 23, 2007. Available online. URL: http://prescriptionaccess.org/blog/?cat=110. Accessed October 30, 2007.

Goldstein, Samantha A. "Teen body image, the media, and supplements: an unhealthy mix." *U.S. News*, August 1, 2005. Available online. URL: www.usnews.com/usnews/health/briefs/childrenshealth/hb050801a.htm. Accessed August 28, 2007.

Goodwin, Kathleen. "Facts About Dexatrim." The Diet Channel, October 27, 2006. Available online. URL: www.thedietchannel.com/Facts-About-Dexatrim.htm. Accessed October 30, 2007.

"Government Announces Ban on Ephedra." CNN.com, December 31, 2003. Available online. URL: www.cnn.com/2003/HEALTH/12/30/ephedra. Accessed August 28, 2007.

"Green tea (*Camellia sinensis*)." MedlinePlus, U.S. National Library of Medicine and the National Institutes of Health. Available online. URL: www.nlm.nih.gov/medlineplus/druginfo/natural/patient-green_tea.html. Accessed November 13, 2007.

"Herbs at a Glance: Bitter Orange." National Center for Complimentary and Alternative Medicine (NCAM), August

2007. Available online. URL: http://nccam.nih.gov/health/ bitterorange. Accessed November 13, 2007.

"Herbs at a Glance: Ephedra." National Center for Complimentary and Alternative Medicine (NCAM), November 20, 2006. Available online. URL: http://nccam.nih.gov/health/ ephedra. Accessed August 23, 2007.

"Herbs at a Glance: Green Tea." National Center for Complimentary and Alternative Medicine (NCAM), May 2006. Available online. URL: http://nccam.nih.gov/health/ greentea. Accessed November 13, 2007.

"How Can I Lose Weight Safely?" TeensHealth, The Nemours Foundation, October 2007. Available online. URL: www. kidshealth.org/teen/food_fitness/dieting/lose_weight_safely. html. Accessed November 13, 2007.

"How many calories are in all foods?" FitDay.com, 2006. Available online. URL: www.fitday.com/webfit/calories/ calories.html. Accessed November 13, 2007.

"How to Avoid Portion Size Pitfalls to Help Manage Your Weight." Centers for Disease Control and Prevention (CDC), May 22, 2007. Available online. URL: www.cdc. gov/nccdphp/dnpa/nutrition/nutrition_for_everyone/ healthy_weight/portion_size.htm. Accessed November 13, 2007.

"I really really hate my body!!!" LiveWire Network: Teen health hygiene & fitness, June 3, 2007. Available online. URL: www.golivewire.com/forums/peer-nnatey-support-a. html. Accessed November 13, 2007.

"Is the Alli Diet Pill Right for Me?" KidsHealth, The Nemours Foundation, June 2007. Available online. URL: www.kidshealth.org/teen/nutrition/weight/no_alli.html. Accessed August 23, 2007.

Ives, Nat. "After a pitcher's death, marketers of dietary supplements try to dodge the taint of ephedra." *The New York Times*, March 17, 2003. Available online. URL: www. nytimes.com. Accessed October 30, 2007.

Katzman, Martin A., Leslie Jacobs, Madalyn Marcus, Monica Vermani, and Alan C. Logan. "Weight gain and psychiatric treatment: is there a role for green tea and conjugated linoleic acid?" *Lipids in Health and Disease* 6 no. 14 (May 3, 2007). Available online. URL: www.pubmedcentral.nih.gov/articlerender.fcgi?artid=1876457. Accessed November 8, 2007.

Kolata, Gina. "How Fen-Phen, a Diet 'Miracle,' Rose and Fell." *The New York Times*, September 23, 1997. Available online. URL: www.nytimes.com/specials/women/warchive/970923_1080.html. Accessed October 30, 2007.

"Learning About Health & Illness: Pyruvate." EBSCO Publishing, available through Massachusetts General Hospital, Blum Patient and Family Learning Center, 2006. Available online. URL: http://healthgate.partners.org. Accessed November 13, 2007.

"Learning About Health & Illness: Vitamins & Minerals: Focus on Chromium." EBSCO Publishing, available through Massachusetts General Hospital, Blum Patient and Family Learning Center, 2006. Available online. URL: http://healthgate.partners.org. Accessed November 13, 2007.

Levine, Shari. "Smoke and Mirrors." GirlZone, 2007. Available online. URL: www.girlzone.com/insideout/SmokeAndMirrors_io.html. Accessed: November 13, 2007.

"Love Your Body." Something Fishy, 2007. Available online. URL: www.something-fishy.org/reach/bodyimage.php. Accessed November 13, 2007.

McGee, Susie. "Guarana Weight Loss Pill." LoveToKnow, October 24, 2007. Available online. URL: http://diet.lovetoknow.com/wiki/Guarana_Weight_Loss_Pill. Accessed January 2, 2008.

"Media's Effect on Girls: Body Image and Gender Identity." National Institute on Media and the Family, September 6, 2002. Available online. URL: www.mediafamily.org/facts/facts_mediaeffect.shtml. Accessed August 28, 2007.

"Metabolife Ultra Weight Management." Available online. URL: www.metabolife.com. Accessed August 23, 2007.

Murphy, Ann Pleshette. "Anorexia Striking an Increasing Number of Boys." Good Morning America (ABC News), February 24, 2006. Available online. URL: http://abcnews. go.com/GMA/Health/story?id=1654439. Accessed August 28, 2007.

"Ox Like Hunger." Teenhelp.org Support Forums, November 28, 2006. Available online. URL: http://groups.teenhelp. org/showthread.php?t=65870. Accessed November 13, 2007.

"Parents Make a Difference!" Southwest Wisconsin Youth Survey, University of Wisconsin Extension, February 2004. Available online. URL: www.grant.uwex.edu/tap/documents/ TeensandPeers1.pdf. Accessed August 28, 2007.

"Phenylpropanolamine (PPA) Information Page." U.S. Food and Drug Administration, December 22, 2005. Available online. URL: www.fda.gov/cder/drug/infopage/ppa. Accessed August 23, 2007.

"Popular Weight-Loss Supplement May Have Nasty Side Effects." ConsumerAffairs.com, February 1, 2006. Available online. URL: www.consumeraffairs.com/news04/2007/02/ cla_side_effects.html. Accessed August 23, 2007.

"Portion Distortion! Do You Know How Food Portions Have Changed in 20 Years?" National Heart, Lung and Blood Institute (NHLBI), National Institutes of Health (NIH). Available online. URL: http://hp2010.nhlbihin.net/portion/ index.htm. Accessed November 13, 2007.

"Prescription Medications for the Treatment of Obesity." Weight Control Information Network, a service of the National Institute of Diabetes and Digestive and Kidney Diseases, November 2004. NIH Publication No. 04–4191. Available online. URL: http://win.niddk.nih.gov/publications/ prescription.htm#questions. Accessed January 3, 2008.

Relacore. Available online. URL: www.relacore.com. Accessed November 13, 2007.

Rogers, Sabrina. "Carb & Fat Blockers." AskMen.com. Available online. URL: www.askmen.com/sports/foodcourt_100/138_eating_well.html. Accessed November 13, 2007.

Roker, Al. "Should teens risk gastric bypass surgery?" Dateline NBC, October 30, 2005. Available online. URL: www.msnbc.msn.com/id/9851183. Accessed January 3, 2008.

Rouvalis, Cristina. "Excessive weight training in boys raises eyebrows." *Oakland Tribune*, November 23, 2003. Available online. URL: http://findarticles.com/p/articles/mi_qn4176/is_20031123/ai_n14563973. Accessed August 28, 2007.

Saper, Robert B., David M. Eisenberg, and Russell S. Phillips. "Common Dietary Supplements for Weight Loss." *American Family Physician* 70 no. 9 (November 1, 2004): 1731. Available online. URL: www.aafp.org/afp/20041101/1731.html. Accessed November 13, 2007.

Shomon, Mary. "Twelve Ways to Revive and Boost Your Metabolism." About.com, December 14, 2003. Available online. URL: http://thyroid.about.com/cs/dietweightloss/a/12ways.htm. Accessed November 13, 2007.

"Showbiz Tonight." CNN, December 29, 2005. Available online. URL: http://transcripts.cnn.com/TRANSCRIPTS/0512/29/sbt.01.html. Accessed November 29, 2007.

Shulman, Joey. "Top 5 ways to boost your metabolism naturally." CanadianLiving.com, 2007. Available online. URL: www.canadianliving.com/health/nutrition/top_5_ways_to_boost_your_metabolism_naturally.php. Accessed November 13, 2007.

"Sibutramine." MedlinePlus, U.S. National Library of Medicine and the National Institutes of Health. Available online. URL: www.nlm.nih.gov/medlineplus/druginfo/medmaster/a601110.html. Accessed August 23, 2007.

"The Skinny on Weight Loss Supplements." iVillage Total Health, October 15, 2007. Available online. URL: http://madelynfernstrom.ivillage.com/health/2007/10/

the_skinny_on_weight_loss_supp.html. Accessed November 29, 2007.

Slendertone. Available online. URL: www.slendertoneusa. com. Accessed November 13, 2007.

"Slim-Fast Foods Company." International Directory of Company Histories, Vol. 66. St. James Press: 2004. Available online. URL: www.fundinguniverse.com/company-histories/ SlimFast-Foods-Company-Company-History.html. Accessed October 30, 2007.

Stark, Lisa. "Is a Diet Pill the Recipe for a Slimmer You?" ABC News, April 3, 2006. Available online. URL: http://abcnews.go.com/WNT/SpecialSeriesCoverage/ story?id=1918654&page=1. Accessed August 28, 2007.

"Statistics Related to Overweight and Obesity." Weight-control Information Network (WIN), a service of the National Institute of Diabetes and Digestive and Kidney Diseases (NIDDK), May 2007. Available online. URL: http:// win.niddk.nih.gov/statistics/index.htm#preval. Accessed August 28, 2007.

St. Lifer, Holly. "How to Lose Your Spare Tire." *AARP Magazine*, July & August 2007. Available online. URL: www. aarpmagazine.org/health/belly_fat.html. Accessed October 30, 2007.

Stolberg, Sheryl Gay. "U.S. to prohibit supplement tied to health risks." *The New York Times*, December 31, 2003. Available online. URL: http://www.nytimes. com/2003/12/31/health/31EPHE.html?ei=5007&en=3390b7 b2695d54cf&ex=1388206800&partner=USERLAND&pagew anted=all&position=. Accessed October 30, 2007.

"The Supergirl Dilemma: Girls Feel the Pressure to Be Perfect, Accomplished, Thin, and Accommodating." Girls, Inc., October 12, 2006. Available online. URL: www.girlsinc.org/ ic/page.php?id=2.1.36. Accessed August 28, 2007.

"Tyra Banks Strikes Back at Fat Tabloid Pics." ExtraTV, January 31, 2007. Available online. URL: http://extratv.

warnerbros.com/2007/01/tyra_banks_strikes_back_at_fat. php. Accessed November 13, 2007.

U.S. Department of Health and Human Services. "Dietary Guidelines for Americans 2005. Chapter 3: Weight Management." Available online. URL: www.health.gov/ dietaryguidelines/dga2005/document/html/chapter3.htm. Accessed November 13, 2007.

"U.S. Weight Loss Market Worth $46.3 Billion in 2004— Forecast to Reach $61 Billion by 2008." ArriveNet, March 23, 2005. Available online. URL: http://press. arrivenet.com/bus/article.php/612343.html. Accessed August 23, 2007.

Wagner, Holly. "Weight-loss supplement shows good and bad traits." Ohio State University. Available online. URL: http://researchnews.osu.edu/archive/cladiet.htm. Accessed August 23, 2007.

Walsh, Nancy. "Bitter orange: FDA called upon to ban ephedra substitutes." *OB/GYN News*, April 1, 2004. Available online. URL: http://findarticles.com/p/articles/mi_m0CYD/ is_7_39/ai_n5996325. Accessed November 13, 2007.

"Warning Letter for Weight Loss Products." U.S. Food and Drug Administration, October 25, 2004. Available online. URL: www.cfsan.fda.gov/~dms/wl-ltr17.html. Accessed August 23, 2007.

"Weight Loss for Teens." About.com: Exercise, 2007. Available online. URL: http://exercise.about.com/b/2007/06/27/ weight-loss-for-teens.htm. Accessed November 13, 2007.

"Weight Loss in a Bottle?" Center for Science in the Public Interest (CSPI), April 28, 2005. Available online. URL: http://cspinet.org/new/200504281.html. Accessed August 23, 2007.

"Weight Loss: Over-the-Counter and Herbal Remedies for Weight Loss." WebMD, October 1, 2005. Available online. URL: www.webmd.com/diet/guide/herbal-remedies. Accessed November 13, 2007.

"Weight-loss drugs: Can a prescription help you lose weight?" MayoClinic.com, February 13, 2006. Available online. URL: www.mayoclinic.com/health/weight-loss-drugs/WT00013. Accessed August 23, 2007.

Weil, Andrew. "Should You Try Thermogenic Supplements for Weight Loss?" DrWeil.com, January 22, 2002. Available online. URL: www.drweil.com/drw/u/id/QAA29956. Accessed November 13, 2007.

"What Are Carb Blockers?" CarbsInformation.com. Available online. URL: www.carbs-information.com/carb-blockers. htm. Accessed November 13, 2007.

"What are carbs?" Harvard School of Public Health. Available online. URL: http://low-carb.brancrispbread.com/ what_are_carbs.html. Accessed November 13, 2007.

"What is Hoodia?" Hoodia Consumer Review. Available online. URL: www.hoodiaconsumerreview.org. Accessed September 30, 2007.

"Women & Patients' Forums." OBGYN.net, 2000. Available online. URL: http://forums.obgyn.net/pcos/ PCOS.0010/0663.html. Accessed November 13, 2007.

Woodward, Susan. "Boosting Metabolism: 10 Tips That Work." MSN Health & Fitness, 2007. Available online. URL: http://health.msn.com/fitness/articlepage.aspx? cp-documentid=100096731. Accessed August 23, 2007.

World Health Organization. "Sibutramine: approved for treatment of obesity." *WHO Pharmaceuticals Newsletter* (1998), nos. 01 & 02.

Xenical. Available online. URL: www.xenical.com. Accessed November 13, 2007.

FURTHER READING

Clayton, Lawrence. *Diet Pill Drug Dangers*. Berkeley Heights, N.J.: Enslow Publishers, 2000.

Henn, Debra, and Deborah DeEugenio. *Diet Pills*. Drugs: The Straight Facts. New York: Chelsea House, 2005.

Mitchell, Deborah R., and David Dodson. *The Diet Pill Book: A Consumer's Guide to Prescription and Over-the-Counter Weight-Loss Pills and Supplements*. New York: St. Martin's Griffin, 2002.

WEB SITES

DIETARY GUIDELINES FOR AMERICANS

http://www.health.gov/dietaryguidelines

This online publication from the U.S. Department of Health and Human Services offers complete, trusted information on nutrition and fitness, including recommendations for weight management.

SOMETHING FISHY

http://somethingfishy.org

This is a leading online resource for information on eating disorders and treatment.

TEENS HEALTH

http://www.teenshealth.org

The Nemours Foundation sponsors this site, offering information on an array of health topics that are important to young people. Find facts about diet pills and other weight-related issues, and get advice for improving body image and self-esteem.

PHOTO CREDITS

PAGE

14: AP Images

17: FilmMagic/Getty

19: Richard Hutchings/
PhotoEdit

22: Tony Freeman/
PhotoEdit

25: Bill Aron/PhotoEdit

29: Colin Roy Owen/Alamy

31: Brooks Kraft/Sygma/
Corbis

37: Lee Prince/Shutterstock

40: Sue Cunningham/
Alamy

42: Getty Images

54: AP Images

61: Michel Newman/
PhotoEdit

65: Dennis Kitchen/
PhotoEdit

69: AP Images

78: London
Entertainment/Splash/
Newscom

80: Newscom

85: Getty Images

88: WireImage/Getty

INDEX

ABOUT THE AUTHORS

AMY E. BREGUET is a freelance writer whose focus is on educational topics. She has written about health, safety, and related subjects in a variety of formats, many geared toward young people. She lives in Southampton, Massachusetts, with her husband and three young children.

Series introduction author **RONALD J. BROGAN** is the Bureau Chief for the New York City office of D.A.R.E. (Drug Abuse Resistance Education) America, where he trains and coordinates more than 100 New York City police officers in program-related activities. He also serves as a D.A.R.E. regional director for Oregon, Connecticut, Massachusetts, Maine, New Hampshire, New York, Rhode Island, and Vermont. In 1997, Brogan retired from the U.S. Drug Enforcement Administration (DEA), where he served as a special agent for 26 years. He holds bachelor's and master's degrees in criminal justice from the City University of New York.

LAKE COUNTY PUBLIC LIBRARY

3 3113 02763 1557

Ex-Library: Friends of
Lake County Public Library

615.78 BREG
Breguet, Amy.
Diet pills

LAKE COUNTY PUBLIC LIBRARY
INDIANA

DEC 08

AD	FF	MU
AV	GR	NC
BO	HI	SJ
CL	HO	CNL
DS	LS	

Some materials may be renewable by phone or in person if there are
no reserves or fines due. www.lakeco.lib.in.us   LCP#0390